PRAISE FOR *WHERE IT HURTS*

"Sarah de Leeuw spins the grit of life — trauma, missing women, the decay of a relationship — into moving, beautiful prose. *Where It Hurts* illuminates the tragedies, triumphs and poetry of marginalized northern landscapes."
—Emily Urquhart, author of *Beyond the Pale*

"Stark, unsentimental, but tender-hearted nonetheless: Sarah de Leeuw's essays prove that there is beauty in hardship, and moments of real warmth in a place known to be so cold."
—D.W. Wilson, author of *Ballistics* and *Once You Break a Knuckle*

"*Where It Hurts* is a mappa mundi, a map of geographical and spiritual space, and Sarah de Leeuw is an extraordinary cartographer, boldly taking the reader into known and unknown territory."
—Theresa Kishkan, author of *Winter Wren* and *Mnemonic: A Book of Trees*

"De Leeuw speaks passionately for the marginalized, whether it's a First Nations woman forced to hitchhike the Highway of Tears, a homeless man watching his hotel room burn up, or a 15-year-old girl working a truck stop in an asbestos mining town. She draws us into the fabric of towns the guidebooks don't recommend, showing us ourselves woven into it, linking a failing marriage to a toxic landfill. Or the serial killer Clifford Olson and his aftermath to the explosion of Mount St. Helens. We feel how much it matters that our threads cross."
—Meredith Quartermain, author of *I, Bartleby* and *Rupert's Land*

WHERE
ESSAYS IT
HURTS
SARAH DE LEEUW

NEWEST PRESS
EDMONTON, AB 2017

Library and Archives Canada Cataloguing in Publication

De Leeuw, Sarah, author
Where it hurts / Sarah de Leeuw.

Issued in print and electronic formats.
ISBN 978-1-926455-84-6 (paperback).--ISBN 978-1-926455-85-3 (epub).--ISBN 978-1-926455-86-0 (mobi)

I. Title.

PS8607.E2352W44 2017   C814'.6   C2016-905842-5
                                          C2016-905843-3

Board Editor: Anne Nothof
Cover design & layout: Kate Hargreaves
Cover photograph: Volkan Ölmez via *Unsplash*
Author photograph: Mary de Leeuw

Sunday Morning Comin' Down
Words and Music by Kris Kristofferson
© 1969 (Renewed 1997) TEMI COMBINE INC.
All Rights Controlled by COMBINE MUSIC CORP. and Administered by EMI BLACKWOOD MUSIC INC.
All Rights Reserved   International Copyright Secured   Used by Permission
Reprinted by Permission of Hal Leonard Corporation

 Canada Council   Conseil des Arts
for the Arts   du Canada   Funded by the Government of Canada
                                Financé par le gouvernement du Canada | Canadä

 access©  Alberta   Edmonton   edmonton arts council
Government

NeWest Press acknowledges the support of the Canada Council for the Arts, the Alberta Foundation for the Arts, and the Edmonton Arts Council for support of our publishing program. This project is funded in part by the Government of Canada.

201, 8540 – 109 Street
Edmonton, AB T6G 1E6
780.432.9427
www.newestpress.com

NeWest Press

No bison were harmed in the making of this book.
PRINTED AND BOUND IN CANADA

CONTENTS

This book, like so much of what I have ever written, would not have been possible without Mary de Leeuw. Thank you mum, for everything. And more.

WHERE IT HURTS

You know this game, right?

It's played at dinner parties?

After a few glasses of wine?

When we've left the kitchen and the dining room and we're all sitting in the living room and there's been three-in-a-row of those awkward conversation lulls, when saying anything seems too loud so we're all busy saying nothing at all, looking interested in the carpet?

The game where you try to figure out the lie in three guesses or less?

Like this.

I say: In my life I have eaten bear, shark, raw sea-urchin egg, ox-heart, seal, and caribou.

If you guess which one I *haven't* eaten, if you catch my lie, it's your turn to fabricate a story. To tell an untruth.

Mostly people guess bear. Especially if I'm in a city. Bear! You can't have eaten bear!

That's wrong.

I've eaten bear. Quite a lot of bear, actually. Shanks of black bears pulled from the backs of 4x4 pickups, hunks of skinless slopping red flesh chucked onto stomped-down cardboard boxes thrown flat to keep the blood off the paint of the truck bed. Being hauled to the dump by trophy hunters. Meat rescued by my dad. Hundreds of pounds of meat thumped onto the kitchen counter and hacked into manageable wet slabs, chasing off the cats mewling at the fatty scent, wrapping it in newsprint, turfing it into the freezer. Turned into stew. Then fed to the dogs when it became too frostbitten for even our hungry mouths, a strange grey ice-mold that sometimes the dogs would pause over, sniff at before swallowing back in loud gulps.

If no one can guess what I haven't eaten, I get to lie again.

I could say: I have travelled to Seoul, Paris, Sofia, Istanbul, Tokyo, Delhi, and Chicago. One is a lie. It's everyone's job to figure out which place I've never set foot in.

I like the game. I like all the strange truths people keep hidden inside them. How easily a lie can be buried in such plain sight.

i

Before that flight back to Vancouver from Sydney, the kind of flight that makes your kneecaps throb and leaves your eye sockets feeling like they're filled with salt, sand, and lemon juice, I didn't know that planes were sprayed down with fire hoses when they are landed by a pilot making his last-ever flight before retirement.

How the water arches and sparkles in the sunrise of a new continent, how water streams down the plane's windows, christening an entire aircraft, how stewardesses clap and smile and how the co-pilot comes onto the plane's intercom system and announces how proud he is to have accompanied Captain Vincent MacDonald on his final flight as a pilot, how Vince is a good man who's put in more than forty years with Air Canada, how from here on in the only flyin' Vince is gonna be doin' is down to Puerto Vallarta or, shucks, Las Vegas, with his wife and grandkids. How there's a bottle of champagne waiting in the Pilot's Lounge and how Vince is going to have a glass or five even though it's 6:30 in morning, Pacific Standard Time. How by then everyone on that massive Boeing 747 is clapping along with the pretty stewardesses, a few voices calling congratulations, Vince, congratulations man.

Before that flight back to Vancouver from Sydney, I had never held a man as he died.

As he pissed himself lying spread out on the floor of the airport, his wife screaming, screaming, screaming, hang on Murray, hang on Murray, oh god someone help, hang on Murray.

I did not mean to hold Murray as he died.

If I had not turned around as we were all running from one delayed flight to another flight we were worried we might miss, if I had not turned around when I heard a strange choke-gasp ragged breathing a few steps behind me, if I had not turned around to figure out what that sound was that I'd never before in my life heard, I would have missed the collapse, the buckling knees of the unremarkable-looking middle- to late-middle-aged man in jeans, the guy with the red-purple face sweating as his wife held his arm saying slow down Murray, we can walk, if we miss the plane, there's another.

If I had not turned around, I would not have seen the man crumple and I would not have dropped my one allotted carry-on piece of luggage in an attempt to catch him and I would not have been the first person to put my hands under his head, his head I was worried must have really hurt from its crash to the ground, its crack against rock-hard floor. I would not have begun to turn him from his back onto his side, some grey-fog memory from some lifeguarding class I failed in Grade 10 forcing itself into my brain, into action.

Now that I'm holding Murray, I'm talking softly and saying it's OK it's OK it's OK, try to breathe slowly, I'm saying this gently, trying to convince him, but his breath is becoming a high-pitched squeal through windpipes, his face changing from fuchsia to yellow ripped with white-blotching, the spit starting to bubble in the corners of his mouth and I don't know what to do so I am reaching into his mouth and trying to pull out his dentures. Seeing how they are so loose and slippery, I think they must be choking him. I feel the sticky warm wet inside of his mouth, my fingers against the smooth roof his mouth, my fingers fumbling deep inside the mouth of a stranger, trying to make space for breath, people in a circle all around us. I yell: Is someone here a doctor, is someone here a nurse, but there is just silence, a few people taking pictures on their smartphones. So then I really yell, loud, *someone call a fucking ambulance* and that moves a few people.

But. Still. Still there is a silent circle around us, Murray and me on the airport floor. Still his wife is kneeling behind me, except now she's just crying, just crying and crying and not screaming. She's telling me some story about how this is their first vacation away as a family, how they didn't want to miss the flight, how his nickname's Chicken, how everyone calls him Chicken, how he has a pacemaker, how it was just put in, how… is he going to be OK? Is he going to be OK?

How with my fingers pulling out of his mouth, I see the piss pour out of him, stain his jeans and flow a little ways beyond his body down the airport floor, how I feel him jerk lightly, his head against my thigh, his eyes rolling backwards.

How out of the corner of my eye, as I'm feeling all of this, I watch his wife crawl up a little closer, on her hands and knees, and gingerly pick up her husband's rose-pink plastic dentures, with their perfect white teeth that I've carelessly swiped away across the floor, and try to discreetly place them in the pocket of her light blue summery linen pants, the kind so many women wear in airports when they're getting ready to travel somewhere new and warm for holidays.

ii

We were, well, let's see: how would you put it?

New to each other?

Dating?

Yes. I suppose we'd just started 'dating' — if that word can apply to two people in their late 30s and late 40s, circling each other like dogs of previous owners who'd occasionally taken to kicking them in the ribs. New to each other and still a bit bruised. Skittish and snarling from time to time. Waiting for the boot.

We were settling into each other, sitting next to each other on my couch. Breaking up the quiet moments with chirpy quips. The way people do who don't yet know each other well, who haven't yet lapsed into silence being a warm comfort. We are waiting for a friend of mine, a woman you've never met. You've told me about your nervousness, you being the man from Toronto, a city man, a southern man, a new man to me.

My friend is the coroner in a town 600 kilometres away. Down the highway. She also goes into all the reserves, all the tiny little places along massive northern rivers with oolichan runs and orcas, with seals and grizzly bears. A few years ago most of the places were fly-in only. Now a paved highway reaches right up and inside them. Totem poles for corner posts on bridges that the Ministry of Transportation and Highways inspects.

It's all new, says my friend when she arrives, after she's turned down a glass of wine or a beer 'cause when the body she's accompanying is brought into the hospital, when she has to leave my house to talk to doctors and police, she doesn't want even the tiniest bit of anything clouding her judgment.

Do you remember when we used to go in and talk to the kids in the high schools up in those reserves? she asks me. How those poor kids were like five or seven years behind with their fashions, still wearing acid-washed jeans in, like, the late 1990s, thinking they were cool? Hell, with no TVs, no movies, how-the-fuck were they to know otherwise?

She and I are laughing now.

Remember how we used to meet with them, to talk about safe sex and HIV, down on the wharves where they hung out smoking Players Light and eating dried half-smoked sockeye salmon like it was potato chips?

You remember?

Oh yeah, I remember.

And then I remember, with her, about the time that she and I worked together with that woman with the six kids who'd all been taken away, and how the woman's husband later killed her, stabbed her in a bad-drunk fight.

And that really beautiful young woman, from Pakistan, you know the one, my friend asks me, her fiancé owned the pub on the way to Prince Rupert, but remember how bad he used to beat her? Would strangle her 'till she passed out and then when she woke up he'd tell her she imagined the entire thing? She'd come into the transition house where we worked, with a purple ring of bruises around her neck, and we tried to tell her she had to leave that asshole, but then she just got so tired, so tired, and she was scared of being on her own, with no money, no family, no one who'd believe her, so she hung herself in the basement of her nice house. Remember?

Or what about that woman from Russia? The one that guy who owned a logging business found through one of those Eastern European Exotic Women online dating services and married over the internet. How she moved out here from St. Petersburg with her cat (what the fuck was that cat's name again?) wanting a better life 'cause she was getting nowhere fast as a florist, but then how, after a while, the guy got sick and tired of her. She was lousy in the sack, didn't talk proper English, and was a shit cook. How he made her live in the doghouse out back, in the fenced-in run where he kept eight German shepherds that kept her warm 'till a neighbor finally called the cops and said: Even some Russian whore shouldn't have to live like that. Remember?

Oh yeah, my friend remembers too, and yes, we know it's fucked up, but we're still laughing when we're telling each other these stories, her waiting for the body that's coming down the highway in a temperature-controlled van.

We laugh about the time we're talking in another local high school, one that's looking pretty good 'cause mostly the kids just drink beer and smoke the odd joint, but Jesus Christ, I ask her, do you remember that day when we're talking about bullying? About homophobia? How we're being all serious and wanting to educate against hate? How that one kid had about a billion words for queer, for fag, for homo? Bushwhacker, beaver-sucker, log-pole jammer, fell'a-buncher, mooser, fox-skinner? Piledriver? You know, like the tugboats do. What the fuck?

We're really laughing now, thinking of how those words don't make any sense. Except they do. Here. Here in these tiny logging towns they're the words kids use to hurt each other, to make each other feel like shit.

Then you say: It's all changed.

You're glad you're gone.

It's really bad now.

Up in the reserves, the boys are hanging themselves with garden hoses. The cheap plastic green ones. If the hoses have never been used to water lawns, which mostly they haven't you say, they stay soft and pliable even in the really cold winter months. The boys, some as young as seven, do it out back of their homes. Mostly from the beams on the bottom of the decks. Mothers find their sons strangled with garden hoses.

After my friend's pager has gone off, after she's been called to the hospital, after she's left, I turn to you, you who is still new to me: yes, remember we're still new to each other. Still wounded. Remember I don't yet know you that well.

Remember that you grew up in Toronto, that you'd not ever set foot in an Indian reserve until you met me. Remember that this is not unusual for many Canadians. Remember that you did not know me when I was a women's centre coordinator, when later I worked in a prison for women. The places where I learned to laugh about these things.

I should have read your silence better. I should have understood that these were things beyond your imagination. Places that hurt too badly to laugh about.

Years later, when we know each other well and are able to sit comfortably in silence with each other, you tell me that night changed everything about the way you understood the world.

In the summertime, in the Okanagan Valley, as people are watering their gardens and setting up sprinklers, thin snakes of bright green garden hoses unfurling across gently sloping lawns, you want to cry. You have begun to understand things you never dreamed of knowing.

iii

Here is what I am thinking on that early February evening when it really has to be below -20 and maybe even planning on getting colder.

I am thinking blue.

Blue. Blue. Blue blue. Breathe. Stroke. Stroke. Blue. I am thinking: Swim harder, remember to reach, reach, twist from the hip, swivel shoulder, kick from *above* the knees not with the knees, use your thighs, count one-two-three, now breathe right, count one-two-three, breathe left. Reach out. Bulkhead. Touch, turn, push off. Blue. Stretch. Kick. Breathe.

I don't know how to flip.

I can't effortlessly touch the bulkhead so my fingertips are against gritty white paint for only the briefest of a second to begin a flip. That graceful beneath-surface somersault my swimming partners have all perfected. So when I touch the bulkhead, I stop. Full stop. When I reach that floating fibre-glass island that cordons off the shallow end from the diving end, that movable heavy hollow block that is carefully slid aside during adult morning swims so the entire 50 metre pool is opened up, I pause. Yes, maybe it's just two or three seconds. But I need to reposition myself. Then I kick off again, soles of feet flat against the bulkhead for just a second or two. Sometimes I think I feel it move a little behind me, shifting ever so slightly in the water, in my wake, as if it wishes I would stay a little longer.

This stopping and then going slows me down. I will never be a swim racer. While I'm telling you what I can't do, I might as well confess that I don't know how to do the butterfly stroke and I can't manage more than 25 metres of breaststroke. Hands drawing backwards and down towards my hips, a motion as if

I'm trying to part the water in front of me, knees up, kick out and back, glide. Like a frog. It should be simple. But I can't coordinate it.

And I never keep track of distance.

Sure I know I cover a little over one kilometre in half an hour, but that's about it. I simply swim from one point on the clock to the next.

Half an hour. Blue. Stroke. Breathe. Muscle and water, muscle and water. Bulkhead. Pause. Push off. Blue. Blue. Blue.

Outside the sky is greying.

I swim after work in the winter. It's too cold to run. I catch sight of the sky on my even-numbered laps: 8...12...14...20.... When I'm breathing on the right-hand side. It will snow again tonight. There is already an almost acre-deep pile of snow on the ground at the edge of the aquatic centre where I'm swimming my laps. A parking lot full of snow shot through with gravel is piled higher than two houses. It gently inclines from the edge of the pavement to the tops of Engelmann Spruce that circle the backside of our Canfor Pulp Mill funded small northern town's multi-purpose recreational centre. All winter long, for almost seven months straight, dump trucks deposit the snow cleared off the roads onto this parking lot. A bulldozer carefully forms it into a massive isosceles triangle, grey and dripping. Pitted and scarred. Young men get stoned and rev their diesel powered Arctic Cat sleds up and down it in the middle of the night. People in the suburbs near the aquatic centre call the cops. Little boys dream of growing up.

Winter in this town is all cold stench of diesel, gravel, and snow.

I swim through winter.

I'm at twenty-five minutes on the clock when the whistles start up. They sound like a series of sharp bird-call screams shot from a mid-sized gun. Loud. But not deep. Like nothing I've ever heard.

Breathe. Breathe. Blue. Against the bulkhead. Head above water. More whistles. Piercing pops. Short bursts. People are making their ways to the edge of the pool. Treading water in an expectant line by the ladders carved into the pool's edge at regular intervals, slowly pulling themselves on deck.

Young lifeguards are pulling off their bright red polyester T-shirts, exposing their dry bathing suits, all the while breathing short pops of breath into the silver whistles worn like rings on the knuckles of their left hands.

The stereo system that normally broadcasts an eazzy-listenin' local radio station has been turned off. The jets in the hot tub have been turned off. No one is speaking. Everyone is waiting to understand what is going on, following each other, confused.

Everything in the aquatic centre is still. The surfaces of the pools are calm. Condensation slides down the windows behind the small installation of plastic fir trees with a dusty fake squirrel in them. The lip of the waterslide drips.

We must number more than a hundred people, all standing in wet lines circling the kiddie pool, the wave pool, the pool with dedicated lanes for laps, the hot tub: hundreds of us dripping. Hair plastered back, goggles askew, water wings slipping low towards children's wrists. We are lost without our flip-flops or our towels, bewildered animals herded away from our soaking, our swimming, our sliding, our splashing.

The whistles stop. The lifeguards, with military precision, align themselves evenly at regular intervals along the biggest pool's edge. They lift their arms in unison. Fingertips pointing skyward, backs slowly curving forward, heads towards surface of water, they dive. Down. Lines of bubbles, white jet streams through blue, along the bottom of the pool, they're swimming, arms sweeping out. Towards the bulkhead. We watch them underwater, otherworldly. They surface, faces milky metallic as they break the water's skin for deep swallows of air. Then they're diving again. They're diving under the bulkhead.

It must be black inside the hollow guts of this floating island, with just inches of airspace, like a bowl turned upside down in a sink of water. We watch the lifeguards go down, under, we lose sight of them, they pop back out, nothing to show.

While the guards are underwater, the entire aquatic centre seems to settle into a perfect thick silence. Like the morning of a season's first snow. When the world is muffled.

The high-pitched whistles have left a ringing in my ears.

Then. Then from a corner of the aquatic centre: Joshua! Joshua! Joshua! A choked sob, a cry that sounds like it's escaping from under a hand held tightly over a mouth. A pale woman with a wet misshapen cotton T-shirt hanging over her bathing suit, the kind of T-shirt women wear to the pool when they're embarrassed about the way their bodies don't tuck neatly into spandex, into women's Speedos, into Nike or Adidas acrylic racebacks. Insecure and self-conscious. Afraid of being mocked, covering themselves.

He was just there, *just there*, he was JUST there, I was watching, I didn't turn away for very long, Joshua, Joshua, Joshua, listen to mommy, you have to come out, you gotta quit hiding, you gotta quit, come out Joshua, quit yer playin' around.

We are all wet. Shivering. We are supposed to be swimming. Floating.

Breathe, breathe. Stroke. Blue. Muscle. Breathe.

Outside there is that pile of snow almost an acre deep. All winter, the weight of it presses down on the parking lot's pavement. Anything under that snow suffocates, drowns.

Breathe.

Inside, on this winter evening, standing on the pool deck, I inhale a sharp bleachy scent of chlorine, my hands hanging slack just below my hips, touching nothing.

iv

I'm forty years old when I finally answer that question we're all asked about a billion times during our lives: If you had just one wish, and if you knew it would come true, what would it be?

I don't even remember the first time I'm asked the question.

Maybe it's in Grade 3, by my pleasant and baby-faced French immersion teacher who, when I look back on it, I'm pretty sure had a latent desire to be a Greek philosopher or something. Or at least to impart deep philosophical thinking skills to his seven-year-old wards. He was the first and last male elementary school teacher I ever had. Monsieur Longe. A little bit pudgy with thick dark hair worn in a foppish swirl over his eyebrows. He'd blow upwards from an extended lower lip when he was a bit exasperated. I remember this because I was the kid in the class who didn't want to limit myself to just one wish. Why only one wish? How do you know it's going to come true, for real? What if it doesn't? Do you get to make another wish? Can I decide later?

Lower lip extended. Dark hair moving in the slight wind of his exasperated exhalation. He once sat me aside for an hour after I'd tried to rat out some other little girl for stealing cookies from a sucky little boy I had a crush on because he cleaned up the medicine balls after gym class and refused to play 'chase the girls' at recess.

You must be loyal to those around you, I remember Monsieur Longe saying. Unless they have done something truly and terribly, terribly, wrong, it is never a noble thing to tattle-tale on those upon whom you rely.

I remember just staring at him. Hating the little girl who I'd tried to rat on even more than I did before tattling on her.

I guess I'm also probably asked the question in Grade 7 by the girls I try to be *best friends forever* with, the BFF girls who mostly all end up pregnant by Grade 10 and by then I've moved to a different city anyway. Where I think I recall it being the kind of question high school boys asked at gravel pit parties when we're mashed together on the open tailgates of their dads' pickup trucks and when I'm so drunk on Silent Sam vodka that all I want to do is puke and, anyway, I'm pretty confident they don't give a shit about the answer but just want to feel my tits.

By the time I'm in university, the guy I end up spending almost half my life with asks the question a few times, but in a sort of convoluted way that rolls around for a bit before he spits it out when we're stoned and he's talking deep, having conversations with me about existentialism and the metaphysical poets — about which I know nothing but pretend to. Being stoned and in our undergraduate degrees means the question comes out as a really focused meaningful inquiry. But…really. *Really.* Imagine there is one thing, one thing, you could *just wish for,* I mean something that might even change the whole world. Everything about it. You could make that wish. And it would happen. What would you wish? Imagine? What would you do with that, like, that total power?

I never had an answer. And we didn't work out as a couple.

Then, last summer, the answer came to me. It's so fucking straightforward I can't quite believe I didn't come up with it back in Grade 1. Certainly by the time I hit junior high school, and for sure by the time I was in university, I definitely should have known the answer.

Here it is.

I wish people never, and I mean ever, set other people on fire.

Pretty simple.

When you think about it.

I wish that no one, ever again and so long as the earth is turning on its axis and the sun is rising and setting, wakes up and then, sometime later like maybe after dinner or even maybe after making breakfast or maybe after chatting with someone they love, like their mother or a close friend, goes out and sets another human being on fire.

You know, by dowsing that other human being with gas and then flicking a lit match onto them. Waiting for the *woooooofffff* sound of flesh going up in flame, the charred burned hair smell that would be the first stench to rise off the burning person, screaming in pain, trying desperately to slap out the roasting sizzling flames wrapped around their face.

I really do think the world could be a better place if my one wish came true. I think there'd be less hurt.

The way I came to my one wish was like this: It's a late spring afternoon and I'm kind of procrastinating on doing things like raking up last year's rotten leaves off the back lawn. So they're probably killing any chance for new green grass to pop up come the early days of summer. But I decide anyway to have a look at online news stories from the *Terrace Standard*. That's the at-one-time-twice-a-week but now just once-a-week-because-of-no-advertising-revenue newspaper published in the town where I graduated from high school. Where my parents still live. Where, when I go "home" and to the grocery story with mum, everyone seems to know us and people I don't even recognize invite me over to their houses for dinner.

Anyway.

There's this photograph on the *Terrace Standard*'s webpage of a man with festering scabs and blisters all over his face, his eyes kind of glued shut with puss. The headline reads "Terrace homeless man burned and robbed." The story goes on to tell me that a homeless man was the victim of an assault that involved him being pushed to the ground, burned, and then robbed. Apparently the 48-year-old man was intoxicated and walking to the men's shelter operated by the K'san House Society.

I worked for the K'san House Society, years ago.

I think of that.

I think of the men and women I once worked with. I read more. I read that at approximately eleven p.m. three men pushed the man to the ground. The story says the police have concluded that the three men held him to the ground, stole his 26-ounce bottle of Smirnoff vodka and some money, and then doused him with lighter fluid and lit him on fire.

The story says the police deduced that the man's face and hand were burned because he was looking at the thieves while trying to stop the burning.

I think about this for a long time. I think about how those three men had the guy's booze, the little bit of money that a guy with no home to call his own would have had on him, how it was a three-to-one fight, how they'd shoved the guy to the ground, and how, still, they decided to light him on fire. Even after all they'd done. An afterthought. An add-on. A 'some-thing extra' that I wonder if even they can explain.

The three guys are in their twenties. Young. Through his burning eyes, the homeless man recalled seeing that one of the men who helped light him on fire was wearing a brown suede jacket.

I think about that too. Is a brown suede jacket the kind of specific article of clothing someone picks out of their closet the late-May night that they head off to set another human being on fire? The evening that will see them inhaling air floating off the charred burning flesh of a fellow person they have just set ablaze?

The story finishes up with some final words from the cops: Do not be vulnerable by being alone, intoxicated, and carrying valuables and money. Be aware of your surroundings. Avoid parked cars, dark alleys, and other dark areas such as bush. Be safe.

I close my unburned eyes, my unscared unscathed eyes and think about how safe I am. How stone-cold sober I am, how I am aware of my surroundings, how I get to avoid dark alleys and other dark areas such as bush just because I'm impossibly fucking lucky, and for no other reason at all other than that. Blind luck.

I close my eyes more tightly and I wish, I wish with all my might that my one wish might come true. I wish people never set other people on fire. My eyes ache, I'm wishing that hard.

v

You were a young mother in Fort St. James before the road through the Indian reserve on the edge of town was paved. Two communities touching, one all paved and moneyed-up with cattle, clear-cutting, and mining. Ranchers in good trucks, diesel engines, front end loaders and eighteen-wheelers rattling to life at four a.m. in tidy driveways leading up to double-wides. Septic ponds out back, tethered dogs that don't bark too much, a corral off to the side with horses and that clean scent of hay-fed shit that warms the ground in winter, almost breathing, the steam rising through settling snow, moist circles of brown earth.

When you first drove into town, through the Nakazd'li rez, your husband pulled over on the side of the road and said: Like it? Our new town?

You believed him.

When you tell the story you say you felt a jagged ripping at the front of your throat, tears welling up. Holding your one-month-old against your breasts, warm, you stared out from the passenger seat at the cracked-and-duct-taped-over living room windows with faded wolf-face-embroidered synthetic blankets and bath towels hung up for curtains. At the heaps of rusting cars and snowmobiles with shot-up beer cans resting on their handlebars. At the dogs running around with teats almost dragging on the ground. At the trikes chucked in ditches, at the kids' bright yellow Tonka trucks crumpled under sharp corners of engine blocks that seemed to have been dropped from the sky. At the strange bent wood frames in front of everyone's houses that you didn't yet know were for tanning moosehides. At the small smoke-stained shacks with doors flung open that you don't yet know are where thousands of salmon will be dried next year, muscly pink meat casting shadows towards Stuart Lake.

You've never seen a town like this. You don't want to live here.

There are so many Indians. You close your eyes.

Your husband laughs, starts the car and tells you he is joking. You're in the Indian reserve. Not the real town. This is Federal Government land. They don't even bother to pave the roads here.

You head into Fort St. James. Less than 500 metres away. You cross an invisible divide. Reserve land to municipal land. A town. Pavement. A small bank. The RCMP station. A Subway sandwich shop. A hotel. A little apartment building with three tidy walk-up stories.

Your husband is here for six months of labour negotiations at the local sawmill. He is a quiet funny man with a slight halting lisp that you love. His hair is starting to thin and you know he's self-conscious about it, running his hands over his skull when you sit together in bed, watching TV late at night. You will follow him anywhere, making a home in these tiny northern towns you'd never heard of when you were starting nursing college down south. He leaves early in the morning, to catch the men leaving night shifts. To speak with the men arriving before the 6:30 a.m. shift. Thermos in hand. Stainless steel lunch box. He never wears a suit. He comes home late. Slumped. You do not know what he does with the men in the mill.

Sometimes it's hard to tell him about your day. How you're exhausted. How in the afternoon you take a nap, praying your daughter will not cry and wake you up, terrified when she doesn't cry that maybe she has stopped breathing. You have no idea what your own job entails, your job of raising a child. You have no one to ask. The house is clean. Tomorrow's dinner is made. Everything is so quiet. There is no traffic in this town.

You vow that every day, in any kind of weather, you will walk the one-and-half kilometres from your rented apartment to the downtown plaza, a descriptor you will never understand. The walk will keep you sane. You will leave the house.

The first time you asked for directions, even the youngest teen-agers told you the name of place markers that had disappeared more than a decade ago. Everyone here seems to know every-thing, forgetting nothing, as if the church were still standing, as if Old Lady Audrey's Café hadn't burned down six years ago, as if you could find your way by turning left where it stood more than half a decade ago but where now there's just an empty lot. You figure it out. You bundle your daughter into her stroller and you push her down the sidewalk and you try not to slip where the edges are cracked off.

On Wednesday, in your third week of being in town, when you've found your way and you have 'milk' written on your grocery list, which offers you a sense of purpose as you walk, a woman stumbles up to you. She is drunk. It's a little after eleven in the morning. She is wearing skin-tight black jeans, steel-toed boots, a black sweatshirt under a man's checkered shirt. A trucker's ball cap. She smiles. She asks if she can see your baby. You would be lying if you said anything other than you were scared. You were scared of the drunk woman in black jeans who you know lives on the reserve because Indians don't live in town. You don't know what you're scared of. You're scared she will kill you. You're scared you will catch something. You're scared of being scared, of not knowing what to say, of every side-ways side-slipping 'drunk Indian' thought you've ever had, of everything you don't know and never wanted to see, of your tiny daughter sleeping, wrapped in the clean pink blanket your mother-in-law crocheted for you. How it smells like Ivory Soap and you're breathing in the leathery scent of rye whisky on a woman's breath on an autumn morning in Fort St. James.

You don't say anything.

The woman thinks your silence is saying yes. She reaches into your stroller and takes your daughter out and holds her. The woman isn't really gentle. But your daughter doesn't seem to mind. The woman hugs your daughter. First she pulls your daughter close to her chest, her mouth close to the top of your daughter's skull where you know the fontanelle has yet to close, where whiskey-breath might simply slip through the thin membrane of newborn skull skin right into brain. Then the woman holds her away, and up, looking her in the eye, bouncing her a bit, not carefully but with something like care, smiling. Hey'ya little baby girl, the woman says. Hey'ya. Then the woman puts your daughter back into the stroller and tucks the pink blanket back under her chin, and laughs. Nice kid, says the woman to you, and you exhale because you've been holding your breath and you don't know what to say. The woman thinks you not saying anything is an introduction. She sticks out her hand and offers to shake yours even though you're standing perfectly terrified still. My name's Cowboy says the woman and you feel the same kind of feeling you felt that afternoon when your husband pulled over on the side of the road on the reserve and told you that's where you were moving to. There are tears biting behind your eyeballs, very close to the surface of your skin.

When you tell this story, more than twenty years after leaving Fort St. James, when your husband's moved onto selling real estate and you own a really beautiful home with granite counters and seashells in little baskets on shelves above the toilet in the bathroom, you're telling the story to a room full of guests your husband's invited over for some art gallery function that's a new part of what he does. That you still don't really understand. Your daughter's in college now, down south. She wants to be an artist.

But here's the thing.

You saw Cowboy almost every day for about six months. She was also always waiting for you on the sidewalk when you walked into town. She was always drunk. After a while, she took to walking with you to the grocery store. You never really talked very much. Once she was gone for two weeks, but when she came back she told you she'd been out berry picking. Then canning jam. You always wondered what her real name was. You never asked. You moved away. You haven't gone back. Not for any particular reason. Fort St. James is only under two hours away, a quick drive west and north down the highway. There just wasn't ever a purpose.

Then, less than a year ago, you were reading the paper one morning.

Fort St. James is all over the national news. Cody Alan Legebokoff, a 21-year-old born-and-raised Fort St. James boy, has been charged with the first-degree murders of three women and a young girl. The newspapers don't give all the details. But isn't it enough to say the bodies were dumped on the sides of the roads off the highway, onto dirt-infused ice under the blackened branches of beetle-killed pines, in gravel pits. That the girls were raped, that the youngest was fifteen years old, that she had some kind of impairment that made her nearly blind? What did she see? What did she see?

You look at the chunky good-looking face of the young man, imagining the rapes. You can't help it. You think of how he had sex with those girls. Before slaughtering them. Clothes tugged off. Excited panting. You think how even the smooth grey stones of Stuart Lake hurt your spine in the summer if you rested back on them in just the wrong way. You hear he dated the girls online, met them using the name *1CountryBoy*. Girls younger than your daughter.

You flip to the back of the paper. It was the strangest thing, you tell us. You hadn't thought of her in years, but there in the obituary section of the local newspaper is a picture of the woman who met you on the sidewalk all those years ago. Held your daughter. Under the photo is her name: 'Cowboy'. Last week Cowboy died. She died in her hometown. Surrounded by family. She will be missed.

You stand in your kitchen and cry. You don't even know why you're crying, but it's important that Cowboy was her real name. Cowboy. That someone named her Cowboy on the day she was born. You think of Cowboy's breath touching your daughter's fontanelle. You hurt in places you didn't know pain could exist.

BELLE ISLAND OWLS

We are running wounded.

Our ankles are not sprained, our ligatures are not strained. Our muscles are not torn, our feet are not blistered. The cartilage in our knees remains sturdy and strong, and we have not ripped a single tendon nor broken a single bone.

So we are running with unnamed wounds.

We are running the makeshift paths and pitted trails that lead to Belle Island. We are cutting down from Montreal Street, just south and behind the baseball diamond and across from the bottle recycling depot, the sound of glass shattering, the crack of a bat on ball, the faint smell of beer emanating from both places.

Summer on the rougher side of a prison town, this eastern Ontario town in the sweat-slick thick days of August in 2005, mid-afternoons humid and heavy like the fiery red bulbs of the fast-growing sumac trees. Like the cracked open pods of the silky milkweed, like the lilac that, elsewhere, is beautiful and heady-fragrant but here, here in the humid air sticking to the shores of Lake Ontario, here the soft mauve lilac flowers are an invasive species.

Vegetation tells us we are summer running. We orient to the coolness offered by oak trees, plan our routes to account for the briary reach of blackberry bushes, avoid trails made narrow by stinging nettles. And we wait for the arrival of evening, that dark bluing of the horizon, a cooling to the wind, a faint mineral smell in the air, slate and granite edging out the warm ripe notes of lilies and strawberries. These are the moments we love. Like the one hour before sunrise and the one hour before sunset, the two times of day we have always agreed to love the best, just before night falls full or just before the morning is complete or real, the two times when the light of our together-world is most perfect. Everything transitioning into the possibility of what comes next.

This evening, like the one yesterday and the one tomorrow and the one the day after that, marks another evening in another day, and we have been together for over five thousand such days, days of dark into light and light back into dark. You and I know each other so well. We inhale together. Each other. Fifteen years of life, together, so that even the inanimate objects that surround us are full of stories, scratched and dented with all the moves we have made. We have transformed the inanimate into animate. Intimate and animate.

The dinner dishes resting in the sink. Alive as we breathe them in, contemplate them.

That off-white bowl with the blue fish painted on the curved inside. The last bowl remaining from a set of four we bought on a street in Vancouver's Chinatown before we moved east. We know, together, that the second to last of the set was broken after using it as dish for dog food. During the four months he needed so much medication and we fed him anything that made him happy. We wrapped his powerful medications and antibiotics, his prednisone pills, in strips of salmon and topped them with balls of truffly milk chocolate. We knew chocolate could kill dogs, but lymph node cancer was killing him more quickly and surely. So why not feed him fudge cake and lamb chops, served in a beautiful blue and white china bowl? That cold early spring morning, not so long before we had him euthanized, not so long before that afternoon when we came home to his teeth clacking and his eyes rolling wildly and the strange muted yips of pain, he broke one of the two remaining bowls. Trying to stand in it, trying to anchor it on the slippery linoleum of our kitchen floor so that he could lick the last trails of blueberry jam from the edge. It slipped away, shattering. We worried about a shard cutting into his soft Malamute muzzle. But there was no blood and he was so happy. Cancer of the lymph nodes is invisible until suddenly it is not. Until it breaks through, ruptures an organ, and euthanization is the only humane thing to do.

The stainless steel chopsticks with cranes winging up the stems. Remember? We bought them in a street market in Onyang, the year we lived in South Korea, our year of persimmons and bitter honey. Our year of sticky rice and spicy chili pastes. Wind through forests of bamboo. Your sadness that I sometimes feared would never, ever, lift. The night of me crying so hard my face was puffy for days afterwards, but there was no one to call as you sobbed in my arms, in my arms despite the hot anger that had smeared our mouths for hours before. There was no one to call because I spoke less than twenty words of Korean and how could I explain that the man I loved said it had crossed his mind to jump from the roof of the 27th floor of the Banchun Hyundai apartment buildings where we lived?

Where we lived, through that night, and where we finally drifted off into terrified sleep, sometime during the one hour before morning was yet real. And everything was transitioning.

Who would I have told, and what answer could they have possibly given anyhow? Make another cup of tea. That smoky flavoured roasted tea with a slight salty tang, like tears. Drink it from a cup glazed in celadon green, a glaze invented in South Korea. Look out over the flat stretch of rice fields. Pretend jumping was a metaphor.

And now we are in Ontario. Having moved and moved and moved. A compost bucket under the sink. The avocado pits that never deteriorate. Like us, we joke.

On the edge of our counter, acting as a weight for our cookbooks to rest against, the bowl of rocks collected on hikes up to glaciers in the Alaskan Panhandle and along beaches on the Queen Charlotte Islands. Weighty reminders that we have left the west and made a new life here, here in Ontario and far away from our families and friends in British Columbia. A new life with the smallest details that we do not want to throw away.

We give no thought to refuse or to decay. We have loved each other since I was sixteen years old. Hauling away our broken hearts has not yet been contemplated.

Instead, when the nights are hot like saunas, we resort to telling stories of western rain forests, the foothills of the Rocky Mountains, the coastal beaches of northern British Columbia. And we stand at the counter in our house in eastern Ontario and we eat nothing but tomatoes dipped in salt for dinner. Juice runs down our wrists. Later we might bathe together, me getting out of the tub first, the water dipping. I dry myself, turning to you whom I know so well, and you will continue to rest as the water cools, maybe reading a magazine. We have relocated and we are adjusting to summers of running along the flanks of Great Lakes we once never dreamed of even seeing.

We run to Belle Island, that small tight fist of wild greenery thrusting out into the slow shallow waters of the Little Cataraqui River. Belle Island, just a few metres off the shore from what is now a park, what was once nothing but marshland. Belle Island, dwarfed in the Thousand Islands Parkway, insignificant because it did not even have the good grace to place itself in the mighty Saint Lawrence, choosing instead a thin tributary. We run through the Belle Island Regional Park, alongside and then past the Belle Park Fairways golf course and driving range. In the park, before we cross the tiny footbridge onto the tiny island, we are running on an old landfill. We are running on an environmental disaster, on a leaching festering wound covered with only the thinnest of scabs. We are running on something that isn't likely to heal any time soon.

The thin scab is bright green in summer. Cheerful. Well-kept fairways, a score card that notes, "On holes 4, 5, and 8, streams and ponds shall be considered lateral water hazards. Drop ball within 2 club lengths, not nearer, hole — penalty one stroke." Hole 8 is near a rise, a gentle bump, in the centre of the fairway. A mound of the discarded, the unwanted and the long since forgotten.

Imagine the city, the first capital of Canada, seven years after the end of WWII. Imagine a post-war city opening a municipal landfill on the edge of town, on a marshland. 1950s city planners surveying throw-away space, space where in autumn there is nothing but the rusty-ochre of cattails and pampas grasses, tannin-stained waters hidden by thick coatings of tamarack needles, a gilded surface cracked by meandering mergansers and geese with wide glossy feathers. The nothing spaces of thorny trees like the common buckhorn, throwaway pine trees, the fire purple of non-native loosestrife, the still wet leaves and tiny white flowers of enchanter's nightshade.

Nothing of any import.

A place to churn up, bust open, and plow into.

This is a small city with a military base at its core. In 1952, having returned from battles like Dieppe and Normandy, military men needed to reshape their lives and rekindle the home fires. Leave killing zones behind and support their wives' desires to install new kitchens, fulfill their own dreams of hi-fi sound systems and televisions. Watch with amazement as milk arrives on the table in plastic jugs and their children start to tune in and drop out while eating Kellogg's Corn Flakes and chugging back glasses of Hi-C orange drink. Sunday afternoons are times for a drive to the dump to the outskirts of town. Backs of station wagons jammed with pickle jars and cereal boxes, different models of microwaves and even small refrigerators as technology changes, as the times accelerate with a dizzying pace that can only be made sense of by getting rid of the old and ushering in the new. There are car batteries to throw away, finger thick thermometers of mercury to chuck out, insulation from the attic to get rid of, pans of oil and stacks of the wife's *Vogue* magazines. There is just so much damn stuff to dump. It's never-ending. That trek out to the landfill on the edge of town, gulls screaming and the ripe ropey rotten smell of garbage in the summer sun.

The mound grows. The runoff grows thicker, viscous veins. It eclipses the little tiny island just off shore. Little fist of oak trees and brambles. Ground littered with acorn nuts, edged in sedges and grasses, punctuated with patches of milkweed, hard pod shells open and exploded, silky feathered seeds expelled, mixing with ragweed pollen and swallowtail butterflies. Monarchs on the wind. The landfill renders invisible the island, the island that the Mohawk Nations up and down the St. Lawrence and Cataraqui Rivers claim as burial ground for the people of Tyendinaga, Kahnawake, Akwesasne, and Kanesatake. The island is quiet, guarding its ancestral bones below the soil, just a few willows and osier dogwood on the surface. In the early weeks of spring both types of trees turn deep, deep red. As if their sap is made from the warm blood of humans. It is rushing into the tips of their branches and igniting the leaves so that Belle Island will come alive again, move into summer, foliage rooted in bones that the Mohawk people quietly, refuse to forget.

Seepage and runoff from the dump pay no heed to people's bones.

For twenty years the landfill grows and the seepage thickens. In 1974, less than a year after my birthday, the landfill has gorged itself to exhaustion and it is closed. Where the shallow waters of the Little Cataraqui River bump against Kingston's landfill, fish begin to die. Bloated bodies wash against Belle Island, on the thin shores of an unmarked graveyard. Bellies up, the mauve-hued veined and semi-transparent skin of their swim-bladders bulging out of their mouths. Caught in a glassy fleshed bubble, a last breath towards the sky.

Sometime after the dump closes down, people begin to say that putting it next to a river was not such a good idea. Piles upon piles of tires produce their own rubbery black heat. Plastic bags circle with seagulls against the white clouds. Streaks of grease tendril out onto the river's surface. The ground is saturated. By the mid-1990s, environmental engineering and consulting firms are studying the site. Undertaking assessments. Writing reports. There are environmental impact studies and landfill site environmental monitoring and operations reports. A site monitoring program is implemented, to undertake long term groundwater management strategies. Groundwater withdrawals are monitored. Discharges and seepages from the site are recorded and analyzed. A decision is made to reclaim the site. The heap of garbage sorted through, all that can be is plowed up, mix-mastered into soils and seeds and left to re-vegetate and then manicured and magically turned into a park and golf course.

The great blue herons, with their glassy glares, with their elegance and aloofness remain standing and never leave. They pull their long heads back into their shoulders, tuck one foot up under a wing, and maintain their balance. Their rookeries are many miles to the west, silver snags in small pools of still water caught in the granite bowls of the Canadian Shield. Here, near Kingston, they watch. Blue beard feathers blowing in the wind, feathers the same colour as the mist that settles on the waters where river meets Lake Ontario. They watch a military town transform into a prison town, they watch walls go up and toxins seep out.

A totem pole, built by men from the local prisons, is raised. Dateless and without memorialization or explanation, it stands as stoic as the herons. Turtles and frogs are rough cut into its trunk, paint peeling and chipping in the rains of the opening years of the 21st century. A merging of east coast and west, men behind walls representing Nations from across Canada, who for reasons unknown and undocumented choose to carve a pole for the entrance of Belle Island Parkway, a pole to watch over the Belle Island graveyard, that still quiet site of oak trees and bones. The environmental assessments have not stopped, even in 2005, but each one concludes there is no concrete evidence that a buried landfill, although seeping and oozing, is the direct cause of any damage to habitat.

Who can say where it went wrong for you and me? Our oldest cat, the cat we travelled all across British Columbia with, who we moved to Ontario with, the cat who waited patiently for us while we lived in South Korea, has a stroke. She wanders in circles, forgets which way she is heading when she's on the middle stair of the staircase in the centre of our house. Sometimes she sits on that stair for hours, occasionally letting out a long wailing meow. We carry her to her basket, to her food bowl. Sometimes I think you never forgave me for travelling, for working back in the west and leaving you alone for so many months, for leaving you alone during the week she had to be put down. You tell me how you took her to the vet's office in the afternoon and she was put to sleep. How she did not struggle but how your heart burst wide open as she gently stopped breathing. Grew slack in your hands. I do not understand why you left her body with the vet, why you said you could not decide if she should be cremated or buried or brought home, so you just decided to leave her. Let the vet decide. But I was away, like always you noted, so how much could I have possibly cared?

And you are right and we have begun to fight for reasons we do not understand. About things that for fifteen years were never worth fighting about. Now there is a sadness to us that is not lifting. A sadness that forgets itself on the middle stair and does not know whether to go up or down, a confused sadness like a creeping seepage. We try to excavate it, try to document the sources of contamination. We spend hours, days, in discussion. We are not skilled engineers and there is nothing so obvious as a twenty-two-year-old landfill as the centre of our contamination. We conclude we will outrun this patch, this going on three years of seeping anger and sadness. We will reclaim the past.

We run to Belle Island, we run in the heat of summer, and we try to outrun the toxins we do not understand. Do you remember the fireflies? Do you remember that night when we waited and waited for the heat to dissipate, just ever so slightly, and finally, when it finally became almost dark, late late into the night, we pulled on running shoes and shorts and we ran towards the island? Down Montreal Street, past the intersection where all the hookers stand next to a cut-rate brake, transmission, and tire garage, past the baseball diamonds, the Legion Hall, the bottle recycling depot. Past the totem pole standing guard at the entrance to fairways built on top of a landfill, along the thin paths crowded by sumac trees, foliage full in the summer season of sticky humidity. We are running, we are sweating and exhausted and we convince ourselves that the heat of today's anger is long gone.

Cross the small footbridge over to the Island. Jog past the small sign, strangled in vines and submerged in leaves, the sign that announces Belle Island is the sacred ground of local Natives, Mohawk territory. A burial ground. Round the corner on the path, feel the temperature drop a degree or two because of the sudden presence of forest, small as it may be.

Tonight, tonight, the island sparkles. Surely this night must be a special night, a night that will never again come into the light like this.

Look at them all, love of my life, man with whom I have grown up, man I fell in love with at the age of sixteen. Look at the lights, look at the fireflies.

Look at the tiny lights darting in and out, around and about. They are spectres with weight, bending and rustling the leaves as they descend and ascend.

Who knew fireflies made sound? A whizzing rush of light, an almost-clicking as they dart past. We turn this way and that and they dart towards us, flashing. You hold out your hand, palm towards the earth, as if you are keeping bones and skeletons in place. Fireflies rest on your fingernails. Their movement is the only sound, the humid heat has made the world silent.

There is nothing in our world but the white-yellow split-second spark of a million or more fireflies. We experience nothing but this surprise moment in a timeless place.

When do we hear their calls? Or do we first feel the slight rustle of wind, the disruption of their powerful night-hunting wings?

We have seen them before, the owls of Belle Island. A duo, mated for life we surmise from our place on the ground below them. Their heads swivel all the way round when they watch us run beneath them, when they peer down at us from their perches high in the thick branches of Belle Island oak trees. They follow our movements, blinking slowly. Once we watched them kill a grey squirrel, snap her up mid-run, torn body swooped through the air. We hoped the killing was quick. We hope nothing suffered. That day, during that run, we told each other tales of owls, to keep ourselves moving, to keep up our running momentum. We recounted every story we knew about owls. We returned again and again to our shared memories of elementary school education in British Columbia, now so far away. A video every child of the 1970s watched: *I Heard the Owl Call My Name.* The story of coastal British Columbia, of where you and I grew up and later met, of islands in mist and fishing villages and Indian reserves. The story of knowing when you are close to death because an owl will call out your name.

Tonight, on this night of fireflies, our run that was broken at first with light is broken again with owls hunting. Our night is split with the almost silent swooshing of their wings, the snapping of beaks breaking the little lights that flash. Frantic fireflies flicking in and out, off and on, and the owls of Belle Island hunting with beautiful accuracy, as if they are trolling nets through the air. They scoop and snap, gorge on sparkle and light.

We should have known, right then, my love, that we could not outrun the things that haunted us, the things we could not name. I remember that night when we stood watching fireflies and owls during that one bluing hour before the full night, a transitioning hour. We stood transfixed in the sparks of extinguishing light.

SEVEN IN 1980

On April 3rd 1980, one day after my seventh birthday, the first woman governor of Washington State declared a state of emergency.

When I was five and one-half years old, I'd gone camping in Washington State with my mum and dad. The year I turned seven, everything I knew about the state, and America more generally, came from that trip.

We drove across the border in a borrowed VW van and my parents explained about nation-states by detailing the reasons our dog had to stay in Vancouver with friends. Travelling into a different country required animals go through a quarantine period. I envisioned Hobo, our black lab-ish mutt, locked in a cage on a wall of cages and I felt worried about borders.

We avoided the Peace Arch and instead crossed somewhere near the tiny community of Midway, about which I recall the smell of sage, crumbly banks of earth fanning off from both sides of the road and, amongst a sea of desert, small parcels of bright green lawn dotted with cherry trees encircling people's houses. I saw for the first time in my life cacti, needly creatures lumping horizontally along the ground's surface. Everything was very dry and the opposite of coastal rain forests, which I knew best at the time.

When we crossed the border, through a thin gate with not much to denote the spot other than a strip of barbwire fence that evaporated quite quickly into shrub, I remember a border guard, a large man dressed in blue, asking me if my mum and dad were really my real parents. He looked me in the eyes and told me not to lie.

I remember thinking about quarantine and the needles of cacti when I assuredly answered that yes, yes, they were *really* my *real* parents. We crossed into the United States and I felt different.

We swam in a lake. I'd swum in countless other lakes, in dozens and dozens of rivers and even in the ocean when we went fishing for smelt in Port Renfrew on the west coast of Vancouver Island, driving there from Duncan where we lived. But during that trip to Washington I developed a never before realized fear of waterweeds. The way they reached up, clung to my bare legs and seemed to snake along my skin. It was the first time my imagination conjured something beyond, something *other than* the weeds themselves. It was the first time I thought about the possibility of things under the weeds, things lurking, things waiting.

My dad gave me a snorkel and mask and together we held our breaths and swam through the weeds, diving right down to where they affixed to the lake's sandy bottom. I saw there was nothing to be afraid of. The world amongst the weeds was all soft green furry light with sparks of rainbow trout smolts, eyes too big for their heads, perfectly still in the water amongst the weeds then darting off so fast it was impossible to see where they went.

Despite my lungs feeling hollow and desperate, I stayed down, down, just turning and turning and turning in the splinters and sparkles of lake light.

My dad and I swam up and down and through invisible spectrums of heat. Cool water near the weeds' roots, warmer water near the lake's surface. He explained fish-camouflage to me, telling me about their light underbellies and dark backs. All fish had creamy white and speckled bellies, like a pale cloudy morning, making them less visible from below, less visible to those looking skyward for prey. Their dark metallic backs made them less visible from above, foiling birds looking down from the sky into the darkness of the water.

During the nights on that camping trip, I dreamed of camouflage and of melting into backdrops. While I swam in the lake, I told myself there was nothing to be afraid of.

Yet the moment I surfaced, breathless and spitting, the weeds again became terrifying. I forgot the lacy light, the bands of warmth. I forgot it all. I touched the water's surface and suddenly I was visible, exposed, the weeds reaching towards my bare legs.

The other thing I remember most about Washington State was the van my parents drove. I marvelled at the orange and brown tartan upholstery on the van's deep and wide back seat, the one I was absolutely not allowed to ride in without a seatbelt when we were driving. I asked and asked to ride without a seatbelt, dreaming of resting full on my back and looking up at the sky through the van's side windows as we drove along in a car that was a house. I loved the cupboards that snapped shut so that our cans of peaches didn't escape when we drove across a border and into a new country, the two-burner gas stove with the blue flame over which my dad scrambled eggs in the morning and, most memorable of all, I loved the thin stream of water that poured into the van's miniature sink and let us wash dishes in a car we also slept in.

Even though I remembered that trip clearly, by the time I was getting ready-set-go to turn seven I was trying hard not to look back too closely at my five-year-old self.

I was moving on.

I remember clearly learning two things on my seventh birthday, that day just before the first woman governor of Washington State declared a state of emergency across the American border. Many other things happened within a few weeks of me turning seven, but there are two things from the actual dinner on the evening of April 2, 1980 that stick with me.

The first thing I learned was that wasps like meat.

The second thing I learned was that moths are furry.

My seventh birthday fell on a Wednesday. I remember the dinner included slices of cold venison that had come either as a gift from my uncle or from a hunting trip of my father's. We were allowed homemade yogurt with greengage plums for dessert. That was it. There was no cake or anything like that. My birthday *party* had already taken place the previous weekend, on the Saturday night, and it had been momentous. The first sleepover of my life. Four girls, sleeping bags lined up on light green foamies, staying up almost all night in what mum and dad called The Wreck Room, a huge multi-purpose cavern with wall-to-wall carpets at the back of the house, added sometime in the late 1960s as a kind of quick afterthought renovation to the 1950's bungalow. The kind of room where cocktails would have been served.

Two, yes two, Twister games could be played at the same time in The Wreck Room, my mother was forever telling my sister and me to 'go play in The Wreck Room,' and my father lined up Bob Dylan albums against the wall under a panel of windows that sometimes leaked.

For my birthday party, my mother baked an angel food cake and bought Neapolitan ice cream, a rarity in a house that was mostly bereft of anything with white sugar. She entertained four girls by setting up an apple-bobbing station in the bathroom, with which we grew quickly frustrated because of the mean bites into the front of our ribs, made by the aluminum tracts in which the glass shower doors slid back and forth along the edge of the tub when we knelt down with our hands behind our backs.

We also played a memory game devised by mother. On a tea tray she arranged thirty different objects: things like a thumb-tack, a spoon, a button, the lid of a mason jar, a pencil, a cat collar, and an elastic. Then she covered the objects with a tea towel, brought the covered tray into where we four girls were waiting, whisked the cover off for ten seconds (during which time we frantically tried to memorize all thirty objects), covered the objects back up again and left the room while we thought about what we'd seen.

The goal of the game, as I recall, was to recite all thirty objects, preferably in alphabetical order, back to my mother when she came to check on us half an hour or so after she'd whisked the tea towel off the tray.

I recall none of us was actually able to recite the objects per-fectly, leaving us all — maybe even my mum — with a strange sense of failure.

The first year that the 1970s came to a literal halt, the year that heralded in a decade of acid washed jeans, shoulder pads, neon coloured sweatshirts, *Flashdance*, spandex, and ghetto blast-ers, was a year of worry. There is no good age to realize that people kill other people, and not just in an abstract, far away, and whispered-around-the-table kind of a way like knowing my Opa and Oma had lived through The German Invasion of Holland and that A Lot of People Had Died in WWII. There is something especially terrifying, though, about learning that people kill other people because your parents warn you about someone killing children really close to where you live.

Just a few weeks after being seven full months into being seven years old, when the idea of being eight was coming into focus and I was allowed to roller skate on the road at the end of our driveway by myself and all I could think about was making my tree house into a museum of rocks, including one I envisioned was rare petrified wood, which people from around the world would visit and pay admission to view, I remember listening to a CBC Radio news broadcast sometime before dinner and learning that a girl had been abducted.

Abducted.

Outside of Vancouver. Really close. Where we'd left our dog and borrowed the VW van for that trip to Washington. Christine Weller was twelve. A feeling like waterweeds on my bare legs slipped up my spine.

I could imagine being twelve.

I watched twelve-year-old girls in my school very carefully, memorizing the special ways they tucked in close to each other to whisper things, all the different ways they swung their hair and fiddled with their earrings, the ways they pulled their shoulders back and dabbed on raspberry-flavoured lip-gloss while they walked around the school in roving packs, studiously ignoring those of us still relegated to the monkey bars, to hopscotch and tetherball games.

By the time I turned seven, a part of me already wanted to be a twelve-year-old girl. I committed the news story to memory, detail by detail by detail. I could recount it. It tingled somewhere mid-gut, held just under the surface. Resting.

I did not ask my mum or dad about Christine Weller's abduction. I did not want them to know I knew about it. Was thinking about it, how it pressed inside my skull like something waiting to burst. How it grew, applied pressure.

Maybe not asking your parents about important things begins around the age of seven, an age when it suddenly becomes clear that what resides deep in the recesses of your brain is yours and yours alone, something that if not articulated cannot be known to anyone.

On the evening I heard about Christine Weller's abduction, I suddenly longed to not be growing up. I thought about before being seven, about lakes and spectrums of heat and light and my father and my mother and everything a seven-year-old wants never to lose.

Five days before we sat down to my seventh birthday dinner, and two days prior to my first sleepover birthday party — which happened to be the night I stopped sleeping in excited anticipation about the party — Mount St. Helens began venting steam.

In school, volcanoes became the topic of conversation. We learned about Mount Vesuvius and families engulfed in molten rock, a dog caught resting at the master's feet, the owner's hand raised mid-air with a bite of food.

One week earlier, on March 20th, our school day had been finished for exactly forty-seven minutes when a 4.1 magnitude earthquake shuddered through the ground, sending the thinnest of ripples across the rinse water in the kitchen sink where I was standing and helping my mother dry dishes, asking incessantly about Neapolitan ice cream: Could you taste the strawberry, vanilla and chocolate separately? How did all the flavours get into one container together? What happened if you mixed them together in your bowl?

And then the shudder.

My mother phoned my father at work. I learned the word 'tectonic'. I learned there was a mountain waiting to burst, bulging on one side, liquid rock itching to rupture out, like the phlegmy hack I'd had with that bout of whooping cough years and years earlier, when a fever had consumed me, hot and disorientating, something deep inside trying to break out of my lungs.

This is what I thought of first when I heard about Mount St. Helens, when the ground shuddered and my mum and I, standing at the kitchen sink in Duncan on Vancouver Island, were suddenly close to something huge, something I did not fully understood, something the radio reports were full of, full of questions and worry.

The spectre of a volcanic eruption hovered first over my seventh birthday party, barely touching down amidst sugar and wrapping paper, and then over my birthday dinner, a family of four looking out towards sky. The table, covered in a blue and white gingham tablecloth with a vase of daffodils on it, was pushed against a window opening onto lawn and then our garden in the backyard. Dad had just turned the soil, the rented Rototiller parked in the rutted damp soil, its blades like fangs in the early April evening sun. The plate of venison sat in the middle of the table, beside the daffodils. A wasp flew in through the window. At first, it landed on the flowers. Then it dropped onto the meat, emitting a slightly irritated buzzing sound. I stopped asking questions about volcanoes and watched the wasp. It tugged at a tendril of rare meat, front legs bracing as it pulled.

Jaws on flesh.

Do they eat meat I asked?

Wasps, my father answered, are carnivorous. Hunters. Sometimes they kill in groups. Mostly they kill on their own.

We watched the wasp, while the volcano waited to erupt across the border. The air was meaty, heavy and pressing.

It was not a volcanic eruption that awoke me in the middle of the night that first night of being seven. There was no reason to wake up. Nothing frightening. Nothing loud. I was not hot, nor was I cold. Yet I awoke. Awoke to shadows wrinkling across my bedroom walls and the moonlight shone in through the window and I turned, for no reason at all, to the glass of water beside my bed, a ring of condensation glinting.

Resting on the rim of the glass was the most ordinary of moths. Smallish. Grey and brown with white spatterings. Inverted, the colour scheme might have been soot on snow. Nothing at all to take note of. Yet I watched that very ordinary moth in the late moonlight of my first ever night's sleep as a seven-year-old. Through the glass, I could see the underbelly of that very ordinary moth. I could see its legs and antenna and the hard little shell of its abdomen, pulsing just ever so slightly as it licked at the thinnest condensation trickles on the glass beside my bed. I noticed for the first time a thin fur covering its body, balanced between moonlight and shadows. I stared and stared and sometime in the night I fell back asleep and in the morning the moth was gone and nothing was out of the ordinary although I couldn't find it anywhere, despite searching my entire bedroom.

Something, or even lots of things more generally, passed. What was present became past. Nothing extraordinary happened, but days of today became yesterday and then became last week. I settled into being seven and forgot it was *not* an age I had been at one point in time. I forgot about six. I set my sights on the next digit, on getting older on growing up on becoming something new all over again. Mount St. Helens held its breath. More days passed. I learned the words Iran and Iraq and I went to school and 1980 was in full swing and things that were no longer right in front of me, immediately visible, seemed impossibly far away. As if they must not exist.

Still, I remember the shudder. I remember the earth shaking sometime in mid-May, shortly after my father had planted the kale plants and broccoli plants and the potatoes in the back garden and the sunlight was getting long again and all I could really think of was school coming to an end.

May 18th. That 5.1 magnitude earthquake.

It was the ash, and not the shudder, that I remember most. The ash and the images of hot mud braiding down slopes captured in aerial photos taken by helicopters and seen on my Oma and Opa's television. Somewhere faraway, yet so so close on the TV. The world was a moonscape, gray snow and fire-eaten branchless leafless trees, snapped and mangled fanning down the sides of a steaming hot mountain. Rivers and rivers of mud. An orange glow.

Lateral blast.

Mudflow.

Ash plume.

That was the part of Mount St. Helens I touched. I hadn't yet been seven years old for two full months, on the morning I went outside with my mum, my lunchbox and school backpack in hand, and I noticed something grainy on the car's windshield. I looked around. Flakes on the leaves of our plum tree. Something like snow, but somehow lighter, on the still exposed and not-yet-weedy soil of the garden. The driveway seeming to move, shift, just ever so faintly in the slight morning wind, ash lifting and re-settling. Next to one of the beams of the side garage, I found a piece of ash the size of a postage stamp, curled like a rose petal. I reached for it, trying to pick it up. It disintegrated with my touch, a smear between my fingers.

Like the sooty dust on a furry moth's wings.

Seven in 1980. Seven and touching ash. Holding onto all the questions I had inside me.

Between April 16th and July 30th the following year, ten children aged nine through eighteen went missing, were reported as abducted, were found slaughtered and mangled across the lower mainland of British Columbia. The news was full of it.

I imagined Mount Vesuvius, families caught without warning, frozen in place.

Children were held so tightly we felt at risk of suffocation, trapped indoors somewhere in the centres of homes, away even from windows, wanting to burst back onto the world while a province held its breath. As if a landslide were balanced above suburbs, waiting to rush down, as if neighbourhood streets and highways were smooth crevasses along which a killer could creep, disappear a child.

That killing frenzy began with Christine Weller in 1980, November 17th, less than twenty-four hours shy of precisely seven months from the day Mount St. Helens erupted. I was seven when it began. I was seven under that ash fallout that covered 22,000 square miles, a thin dusting over all the places where the bodies of children would be found, twisted, as if caught fleeing in panic, as if unable to outrun a volcanic eruption.

WHAT FILLS OUR LUNGS

Your body, had it been found, was worthy of wrapping in silky white strands thin as whispers.

It was worthy of threads that could be woven in warps and wefts strong enough to fight back flames. Your body was worthy of a weaving that Romans would have called a funeral dress for emperors. Although in the end it was water that claimed you, water that refused to relinquish you, your body was worthy of asbestos.

And in the end we have lost asbestos too. We have lost those filaments of earth reminiscent of feathers and eiderdown and we are losing the memory of mining the mineral that wages war against our lungs even though it was once, not so long ago, the mineral that made the town of Cassiar.

I want to remember you. I want to remember Cassiar. I want to call you both back into this world where I breathe, fully. I want neither of you to have drowned. I want to pull the water from your lungs and I want the lungs of this nation to inhale deeply, to remember that it was men with good hearts who mined a mineral that, during its time, no one thought could be as dangerous as we now know it is.

So come up out of the water, come up with your laugh, that insecure sideways laugh of a teenage girl all lanky-limbed in jeans a size too small, hair stripped bare of natural colour and shining elemental with peroxide gold. Come up and stand beside me again, hip cocked to the left, jauntily-sure, as you stare down all the boys passing us in the hallways of Skeena Junior High.

Come up through the two decades that have now passed, come up from the water that refused you a womanhood, come up and ask me all over again to hold your ripped-up plastic-covered three-ring binders all marred with hearts doodled in Bic ballpoint pen.

Come up and help me remember the summer I worked on the Stewart-Cassiar Highway. Help me remember that summer we both thought ourselves invincible and one of us was wrong.

It is the early summer of 1989. For the two of us it is the end of Grade 10. Gravel pit parties and plastic bottles of Silent Sam vodka, bootleggers met in the mall, twenty dollar bills changing hands behind pickup trucks and just the hint of nights that will soon be lit up with pale green washes of northern lights. We the girls of northern BC are coming loose of our parkas. We are like freshwater invertebrates, larva shedding our hard casings and wriggling up onto the surface of social streams, wings still sticky with winter we are ready to become terrestrial beings, darting into sunshine and getting ready to spread beach towels down on the gravel bars of the great northern rivers we live up against. We plan for bikinis. We wiggle into dresses a size too small and several inches too short. We yank down and slice up the already deep V's of our late-80s cut-up T-shirts and we shimmy into bras that make our mothers groan and we go into summertime show mode.

We offer ourselves up to the light and your sunshine peroxide hair is like a beacon of light for boys and men. In a celebration of coming summer you strut your stuff in the clouds of dust that are kicked up by pickup trucks skidding on the gravel laid down, layer upon layer, over the previous months, over the ice and slush of winter roads in tiny northern towns.

Did I ever tell you how envious I was of you? Of course not. To say that would have been to admit something close to love. Love of your tight, tight, jeans, the kind that needed pliers to get the zipper up, the kind that my parents simply vetoed. Love of your cool and easy ways with the boys who drove cars so rusted out we could see the pavement rush by under our feet when we were all crammed into the back seat, when we sparked up joints rolled loosely in our teenage hands that, despite all our bravado, were inexperienced and awkward. Fumbling.

Fumbling like those boys with whom you were cool and around whom you were so, so collected. The boys who we interlocked our hands with, whose tongues we allowed to slick into our mouths and down our necks before they took their swigs from bottles of beer they weren't yet old enough to buy, those boys who drove their cars fast and like it mattered, like someone somewhere gave a shit. Like their lives depended on it, like they were outrunning something mean and haunting and you, you with your sprayed-up peroxided hair, you made them feel like it was all worth it. Like they were running straight from meanness toward you. You, you made them matter. You held out a promise in your fifteen-year-old arms, a promise that even if those boys spent all the best years of their lives busted down by a lumber mill, you would be the woman waiting for them at the end of a long night's shift. You were the promise of the woman waiting to wash the sawdust from their Red Strap jeans, waiting to love them in ways they still only imagined.

I already lacked the knack for that, even in the early summer days of 1989 when the light was getting longer and the snow lines had retreated far into alpine and what had been in early May just the slight hush of bright green had finally blossomed into a horizon of full foliage.

Purple Aster is on the wind. The Skeena River and the Nass River and the Kalum River and the Dease River, rivers that link two summers across four decades, are starting to run fat and full again, thick mud-creamy water swallows up the chunks of ice that just weeks earlier jammed even an idea of free-flowing currents. Things are on the move and every living thing seems to be sighing with the relief that winter is fading.

These same cycles, these same turns of events, would have happened forty years earlier. In the early days of summer in 1949 the nights too would have come later and later as a team of two geologists, Leon Prince and Bill Little, accompanied by camp cooks and pack horses, made their way up the Dease River, up what would one day be the Stewart-Cassiar Highway, up to survey the wilds of the northwest.

I think of the shadows cast by those horses, animals with names that have never been recorded. And when I imagine those pack horses I think of the lines of their ribs and the way that calluses form under hair when a saddle rubs damp flesh for weeks and weeks on end. I think of compasses and pickaxes and tools to record geology, the world classed by rock type, a hunt for elements, a map of minerals. Was it their compasses or the search for terrain easy on the horses' hooves that led them first to that thin-armed tributary of the Dease River, a slip of water named McDame Creek? Water that calls forth the idea of absent women, a creek beside which Prince and Little came across those fields of asbestos, asbestos so thick it's said the geologists thought it could be gathered up with rakes.

As the years unfolded, other geologists wrote the stories of McDame Creek's asbestos, stories of seams and "veinlets" of that furry mineral, something so warm and wooly that mountain goats were said to sleep in it, white hair in white hair. Stories about gold deposits and about the Klondike gold rush and even the years before the rush, stories about panning on the bars of McDame Creek, about the dreams of treasure offered up by the earth to men who took chances and chased the dreams of mining. Prospecting.

So when those pack horses arrived with their geologists in 1949, it was to a sound of hooves crunching through brittle slivery white filaments, the sound of asbestos underfoot.

It was the summer of 1989 when I first travelled up the easterly arm of the Stewart-Cassiar Highway, the arm that branches off in a hard right-hand turn at Meziadin Junction, that old logging camp assemblage of Atco trailers bleeding pink insulation fibres, Ministry of Highways gravel trucks, and families gassing up and buying the kids strawberry milkshakes and plates of greasy french fries. In 1989, the arm of Highway 37 that goes north, the arm that reaches out and snakes up across the Yukon Border, elbow somewhere around Whitehorse, fingertips touching Anchorage and Fairbanks Alaska, is an unpaved pockmarked potholed highway that truckers call a son-of-bitch and tourists buy T-shirts about, T-shirts that read "I drove the Stewart-Cassiar and Survived."

In 1989 I am fifteen years old and ideas about loss are as foreign as countries with names I still do not know how to pronounce. I have accepted a job as a waitress and cook's helper at the Bell II Truck Stop, interviewed for the job in a hotel room in downtown Terrace. Promised to get myself north the following weekend so that come Monday morning I could start pouring coffee into the thick white and green porcelain mugs on tables rested upon by the elbows of truckers making runs from Anchorage to Dallas, truckers who rested long enough to fill up with asbestos in a town that would one day be bulldozed into oblivion.

In those days it was Arrow Trucking that hauled the asbestos, hauled that fluffy white carcinogen in bright canary-yellow boxes and beds festooned with a long orange arrow and great big black block lettering shaking on the torn-up gravel of the Stewart-Cassiar highway. I was heading up to serve the men who drove those trucks, to set down before the truckers thick slices of apple pie, to collect tips from men who trucked in the high-rolling good mining days of the Cassiar Asbestos Corporation, the days of the late eighties when Cassiar had a booming population of 3400 people, when the phone directory indexed people like Walter "Wally" and Lisa Drzimotta who lived at 631 Tagish St., or William "Bill" and Cecile Pratt on 610 Carmacks St. or even, nestled in the last pages of Cassiar's phonebook, Leonard Zimich at 186 Zimmerman St. These people pulled asbestos from the earth and lived upon the streets that are now nothing but an echo in a memory. These were the days when phone lines connected Cassiar to just about everywhere else and all you had to remember was that the numbers all began with "778" and just about anyone could tell you something about whomever it was you were trying to reach.

I remember making my way north, single bag in hand, lonely without even knowing the meaning of loneliness. Up along the gravel roads all girdled in summer-purple fireweed and festooned with the tight-fisted leaves of young Devil's Club still unfurled. Up past Bowser Lake and lilies on black water and along the Bell Irving River, up toward the plateaus of the Spatsizi Wilderness range with a tingling sense of Mount Edziza and grasslands, marshlands, flatlands beyond the arctic divide with grizzly bears and mountain goats and hunters and miners and Indian reserves balanced in-between the Iskut and the Stikine Rivers, a land so huge that even then it made me want to weep, I was rendered so small.

I remember that it was a Sunday I headed up north because the night before had been a party night, a Saturday night sweaty teenage party all full of false assuredness in the gravel pits and farmer's fields at the top of that hill on the western edge of Terrace, the hill that sloped down toward the Skeena River and the hill from which, if you stood close enough to the edge and looked west along the highway towards Prince Rupert, you could see the Kalum River, full-bodied and jade-green, dumping into the Skeena just past the black railway bridge.

I remember it was a Sunday I travelled north up the Stewart-Cassiar Highway because I was still full with the stories you'd poured into me during the Saturday night party, a night of bonfires and revving cars peeling out on gravel deposits, a night when I had spoken with you, you who I envied, you with your swagger and golden helmet of hair. You had poured into me dreams about becoming a teacher, dreams of getting married, worries about when you would finally lose your virginity and excitement about being just two years away from finishing high school. We were going to live forever, we promised each other. At the end of the summer I would come home, back south down the highway and then west to Terrace and we would start school and we would once again take our places in the hallways with lockers beside each other. I would be flush with cash from working in a truck stop, you would be tanned from swimming in the north's mightiest of rivers.

So that Saturday night we pulled early summer air deep into our lungs. We laughed and we knew about all sorts of things that we really knew nothing about at all. We were prospectors full of dreams, sure of the gold in our futures.

That would be the last time I saw you.

I did not know this. I did not know as I made my way north along the Stewart-Cassiar Highway. I did not know when I arrived in what was then a heap of plywood buildings huddled on the edge of the road, a jumbled mess of doors with screens duct-taped down in desperate attempts to keep out mosquitoes, just about half a kilometre downstream from the bridge over the Bell Irving River, a set of gas pumps, an Esso sign that blinked in the night from behind its mud encrusted and flying-rock-cracked plastic siding, a parking lot carved out for the eighteen-wheeler rigs to pull into, nose to end to nose to end, a restaurant of sorts, hard orange plastic booths and a dusty glass display case which contained an array of pies: apple, blueberry, cherry, and sometimes even lemon meringue when we got around to mixing water with the Sherriff brand lemon

59

pudding mix and heaping it into the ready-bake crusts, pulled straight from the freezer, and then dolloped with spoonfuls of Cool Whip, all that custardy lemony goodness loved best by the men who drove bright yellow Arrow trucks. .

I took orders for Salisbury steak and beef'n barley stew. I served fried eggs jiggling and easy-over soft with HP Sauce on the side and a mess of fried potatoes. When the dishwasher was on the fritz and the cook was too drunk to care, I scraped sausage fat off diner plates and rinsed stains left from the tartar sauce that accompanied both Chicken Finger Dinner Number 7 and the Fish and Chips Platter For The Hungry Trucker. I listened to men lament their wives and give tips on how to strap down or winch up the heavy loads they hauled on roads they grew so sick and tired of that all they were left to do was swig on flasks of Canadian Club and tell jokes about Indians, hookers, and whores across the CB radio waves.

I did not know that you were making your way through the last summer days of your life. I did not know that young women died, their bodies pulled under the currents of northern rivers, never to surface again.

Nor did I know that corporations killed entire towns, that when minerals ceased to make profits, mining companies simply pulled up stakes and bulldozed under the family homes and schools and skating rinks and post offices and small churches and corner stores that for over forty years were the things of a town, the places where people fell in love and made love, the places where parents brought up their children and children were brought into the world, where Christmas parcels were mailed or ingredients for meals served to the grieving were bought, the places where lives were lived and asbestos was pulled from the ground and celebrated. Celebrated for being strong enough to ward off flames, seemingly built by a miracle of nature to insulate and keep the families of America warm and snug and then, in September 1992, auctioned off by Maynard Industries from Vancouver. How to measure the damage? How to properly conceptualize the act of obliterating a dream? How to think of that other than as a mass drowning, a forced under, a gasping loss of consciousness. Lost. Never to resurface.

And it still chills me to the bone, to think of you drowning in the Kalum River. I want to ask one favour of the world. Do not take the lives of teenage girls looking only for answers to questions they don't yet know how to ask. Do not take the lives of girls rafting on rivers and do not take the lives of girls who, full of hopes and dreams about a future solid with companies they believe in working for, walk the gravel roads that make up towns built on mines and factories and mills and docks and truck stops.

If only I could have told you then that the world would miss you now. Come up from that summer day, a day that I awoke — as I did every day on the Stewart-Cassiar Highway — at 4:14 a.m. and the sun was already shining and the ravens were calling and I would have tugged on jeans and a sweatshirt, flipped the switches on the coffee pots with filters full of grounds I measured out the night before, and I would have gone outside and swatted at the mosquitoes and blackflies ready to gorge and I would have banged with both my fists on the walls of the sleeper-compartments on the cabs of the Arrow trucks lined up outside that truck stop in the middle of nowhere and just a little ways south of the town of Cassiar. These trucking men are lost now too.

And the day that you were lost, the day you hooked up with a group of boys from out of town, was a day that the sun shone so brightly, so hotly, that it seemed like the perfect idea to tube down the Kalum River. I imagine you laughing; I imagine the lines of your ribcage clear below the thin material of your bikini as you packed your inner tube and plastic shoes. I imagine the sand and gravel under your feet on the bars that jut out into the green waters of the Kalum River, waters just as green as the waters of the Dease River flowing against the edges of the town of Cassiar. I imagine how you would have tossed your hair and how you would have accepted the beers those out-of-town boys offered, how you would have been tough at fifteen, tough like I thought I was hitchhiking back and forth on a highway where women were left for dead if they didn't put out for the truckers they rode with. There are things that pull us down. And there are things we survive, we teenage girls of northern British Columbia, while we watch the girls beside us drown. It is like the life and death of resource towns, some left standing while others are washed away in torrents of progress. If only I'd known. If only I could have told you, as my father had told me, that the currents of the Kalum River are deceptive and cannot be trusted. They are torrents strong enough to kill.

Come up. Be found. Put the grief of your parents to rest, you whose body was never recovered, you who is all but forgotten, you who like the town site of Cassiar is now nothing but an absence.

Come up and let me tell you I survived that summer because the time was meant to come when I would speak you back into this breathing world.

QUICK-QUICK. SLOW. SLOW.

Think of this city as a dance.

A back and forth, leading following, a whirling-rotating-sweetheart-turn-and-occasional-stumbling across the scuffed wood floors at the family Y on a Tuesday night, 7:30 p.m. sharp during the high months of winter. Months of air that take you in their icy arms and cause sharp, almost painful, inhalations. This is the dance of a northern winter town. Minus twenty and falling. Leaves long since fallen, men and women looking for ways to pick themselves up, turn their hearts around, keep their fingers crossed for a come-soon spring while hoping for a cold harsh enough to stop the red infestation of the mountain pine beetle, a cold mean enough to kill, a cold to make life good once again.

This is a town that dances to a beat of seasons that have stopped delivering winters with days of a cold deep enough to kill the insects that choke the veins of pine trees.

This is a back-and-forth town.

But dance, oh dance, dance nonetheless. And think of couples in jeans and T-shirts. Men gussied up in their second best pair of slippery-soled cowboy boots, belt buckles glinting. Women wearing no-scuff pumps and satiny hair elastics. Flushed, they coax their men into a dance class. Oh yes, they promise returns of happiness to their men. Take me in your arms, say these women, take me in your arms.

This is the same thing we ask of this town in which we live. Please. Please take me in your arms, northern town of pulp mills and pickup trucks. Take me in your arms and give me a home and a front door and a back yard and some semblance of comfort carved out of the wilderness, some safety from howling wolves and the birds of prey that would most certainly take us. If only we were small enough, they would take us away to the wilderness by hooking into us with talons and lifting us away, crying in a wind racing through streets that fall dead by dinner time.

A Hungarian man instructs, elegantly holding his lady. Watch them move. Together they just might be a single body. Squared-up and solid. Then floating perfection, hands gently locked. She closes her eyes and he moves her safely backwards.

Keep your ladies safe, he reminds the men. In this dance, it is a man's job to lead.

And this is a man's town, a town of men, a town led by men. So go ahead. Conjure this dance as I tell you about this city. Step mid-swing into the two-step stream. Step into a time of resource town history. Let's begin in a time that doesn't need a date. Know only this. Things are young and lean and there is more that is wild than there is that is tamed. Homes are few, women are fewer. Camps and tents and men are bursting with the same energy and force as the full-flow rivers rushing across the land. Nothing is yet dammed or diverted. There is no possibility that forests might end. No one dreams of days when salmon runs might cease to muscle up the mouths of estuaries, schools of silver fish bunched and bountiful, swimming flesh water-dancing toward the gravel of their birth.

You can start here.

Make your first step (quick-quick).

Step into it, step into the flow and the current of this dance that is all young strong-angled jaws, sinewy muscled arms that carve out miles and miles of road into the bush. Lines sliced into wet moss, fern, and forest. Dreamlines of days in the future, days of damns and power and mills. These dreams fuel men made of tight muscles and tendons, men who wield saws and axes during the day, men who lean against Clydesdale horses for warmth, the hot slick sweating and hardened bodies of horses huffing great clouds of breath as they strain to move lumber along winter logging roads buckling with mud and ice.

Quick-quick, young men who work and break this land. Dance to the beat of sweat-slicked logging horses.

Quick-quick you men who hold in your hands everything that is steel and iron and hot steam that punches through boreal forest. Logging roads. Dance to the patterns that these roads make, dance to the lines and scars that encircle Prince George. Learn to drive these roads, twisting into camps, into lean-tos and then, as the years pass, fold your dancing bodies into crummies if you are a logger. If you are a miner bend into the blunt-headed drill bits and the dynamite and granite and the thick tires of excavators and heavy-duty equipment that breaks open the backbone of this earth.

This is a dance ripe with the smell of men's breath and sweat. Oh how you men lean in close to the edge of our necks. You catch your own breath. We step in toward you. Into the beauty of muscled arms. In this dance, which is this city, everything is a sweet raw choreographed whirling, a town on the edge of becoming. Country and western tunes, the clip-clopping one-two, one-two, one-two of lyrics rolling out and crying on for more. We will cry out for more in the arms that are this dancing city.

Into the arms of the men who hoist chainsaws and make deep cuts into the forest, the wail of metal teeth into soft wood, spruce trees bleeding their sticky pitch into pulp, mills devouring everything that is measured in broadsheets and cubic feet. Into the arms of the men who beat rocks into dust, the earth chewed up, spat out, the arc of ash and tobacco chew. And oh, once these men have arrived we join them, just after those quick-quick early years of the boom that dances toward the bust. How we women in this town miss our men, our chests heaving as our men roll away and dance into the early morning hours of work.

One-two, one-two. Quick-quick with a slow, slow, right-angled slide around the corner, close your eyes and trust your man.

Slow. Slow. These are the steps of a city going soft with middle age. Slow now the dams are in place, slow now the trees are second and third growth and the natural gas is lessening and the fish are disappearing and grasses and cattails are filling in the railway tracks.

These are the steps to a dance that moves to the beat of busted open and flat broke. Slow. Slow. The beat of a resource town curling up around the edges, downsizing and dismantling. Pulling up stakes, closing up shop. The wilting summer evenings of late August, the shutting-down of camps and mills and the slowing of trains and the crumbling shoulders of decommissioned logging roads overtaken by alders, thin saplings that turn the gravel green and return them to forest. Those gravel roads that were once all torn up by tires racing under the weight of 'fully loaded' and heading into the scales.

Slow. Slow. Now the sinewy muscles of once-working men are slacking from the decades of sliding in and out of pickup trucks, from the popping of hoods and the clitter-clatter of tools dropped and forgotten on the shop floor, the pumping of propane into barbeques instead of diesel into eighteen-wheelers. And the sitting, yes, the sitting and the talking about when the money was flowing and the going was good.

One-two, one-two. Slow. Slow. Slowing.

Sitting quietly with hands crossed just below the chest, watching from a couch, a reclining chair, witnessing your wife and children, everything you dreamed without ever understanding you would one day be stooped, like a cringe, watching your body deteriorate from all it has achieved. The slowing of a town built on a boom, the bust unfurling, the belts slackening, the iron rusting.

Think of an economy built on wood, on timber and trucks and an industriousness that means we are all breathing an air thick with pulp dust and the taste the orange flames that spark all through our nights, sour gas flaring, flare-ups in steel pipes that burst like the anger of an unemployed man, sparking and spewing and dancing with the stars cut in the sky above this northern two-stepping town. Oh Prince George.

Think of the hands of men. Think of any northern city with mills at its heart,

Now let me take you back to the family Y on a Tuesday evening, 7:30 p.m. sharp. Let me show you how he stands before me, how he rests one hand just above my hip, curled around my waist, and in the other he cups the angle of my shoulder blade. He begins.

This man of this town built by men.

Did I tell you he once worked the rails? Did I tell you of his broken hands and a body so sore he was once barely able to move? Think of him. Conjure him for a slow, slow, moment. Think of this dance partner of mine, body on the line. Day in and day out. Quick-quick, slow, slow. He salvaged the ties that bind the tracks, lifting tons of creosoted blocks and heaving slabs of slate. Know that he now leads me backward, oh dancing man of mine. Know it is his job to keep me safe.

Let me remind you of the moments I think of the hands of the men who work this town, laying their palms down on the machines that fill our factories and mills, that chew up and spit out the boards from those pine-beetle killed trees, rusted needles all dry and fragile. A red tide bloodying our northern horizons.

Tap your foot. Listen to the beat, the lonesome call of Johnny Cash, the beaten-down love and whiskeyed-up voice of Lucinda Williams, the wails of Patsy Klein and the bushwhacked lands upon which we dance, frozen ground and acres of snow, high gloss sheen leading right up to the parking lots outside the pulp mills, the sawmills, the lumber yards, and beehive burners.

This town is a two-step dance. Quick-quick. Slow. Slow. One-two, one-two. This is a town built for the basic two-step rhythm, a town made for a dance with moves like the 'lady's outside turn,' the 'corner rotation,' and the 'wrap position.'

Did I tell you he once fought fires? Oh dancing man of mine in this two-step dancing town of ours. From creosote railway ties to walls of smoke that a devil might exhale. Body against flame. Hands curled around axes and chainsaws, blistered palms and ash-filled scabs stinging in burning heat. Those are the hands that guide me. They are the hands on my shoulder blade. The hands on my waist, curling in, turning me out, leading me to safety.

This is a man who will throw himself against a rampaging enemy so that it does not eat every last tree, and therefore every last log, that keeps the town of Prince George alive. This man fights fires and salvages railway ties and on Tuesday night he teaches me to follow, he takes me in his fire-fighting hands and during lesson four we move from the 360° Rotation to the Outside Turn to Sweetheart to Promenade and we two-step it right down the centre of the dance floor and I close my eyes and the town around me disappears and I am wrapped in the hold of a country-and-western song and Prince George is tapping its cowboy boot and we are dreaming of the Cadillac Ranch and women, oh women, your men are trying, they are trying to keep you safe like the arms of this northern resource town.

Take me home, one-two, one-two, take me home in those arms that have built this city, arms that have ripped open the earth and hacked down the wilds and arms that are (in a swing and waltz and ballroom citified world) bound to grow slack and passé. Take me home. You with your arms of a two-stepping man in this two-stepping town. We will dance.

SOFT SHOULDERED

This part is true.

It is true because it is named and found. People have investigated and made inquiries. And inquiries result in findings and findings can be documented and published and circulated and so people pay attention and they search for solutions.

Dystocia is the name given to any difficult childbirth or abnormal labour. During childbirth, when the anterior shoulders of the infant cannot pass below the mother's pubic symphysis, when a baby's shoulders are wider than the opening in a mother's pelvic bone, it is called Shoulder Dystocia. Imagine an infant gasping for breath, trying to emerge into the world. Imagine watery panic. Contractions. Bone against bone, unyielding.

The quickest solution is to break the baby's clavicle bones. Reach inside, first one side and then the other, thumb on tiny collarbone, hand grasping around the curve of shoulders, fingers on shoulder blades. And snap. Yes. Snap. This must be done with force and conviction. A clear fracture heals with fewer complications. We tell mothers that their babies will not remember that excruciating pain. We tell mothers that their children will cross a threshold into life with limp and broken shoulders. But the bones will bind themselves back together again and the breaks will set and arms will again stretch out strong. Their children will be poised for running, running, and being alive with breath pulled deep into lungs.

It's enough to make a person cry. With relief.

This next part is no less true.

And it hurts no less.

But there is nothing named or found and so nothing is documented or published. The sparseness of findings and inquiries has resulted in almost nothing and so nothing has been circulated and solutions are slippery and invisible.

No name is given to a child born to vanish. There is no diagnostic term for those who slip into this world born to disappear.

There are no solutions or diagrams or carefully recorded scientific data about the daughters who effortlessly take their first breath, who pull air into their lungs for years and years but for whom each breath is a breath closer to the moment when, on the shoulder of a highway, they will go missing.

This too is enough to make a person cry. With anticipation of what is coming.

And it too begins at birth, the edge of life, a life running and rushing, arms outstretched, towards a vanishing.

So begin with me at the edge. That borderland where pavement ends and soft shoulder begins. This is a land bordered by a wall of green so dark it might be black. At highway speeds, this is how Engelmann Spruce trees appear. Through a car's passenger window, branches blur and trunks transform. Things get hazy and things get lost. The details disappear.

Asphalt dissipates into gravel, gravel touches mud that curves into ditches scarred and slashed by the bulldozers and the D9 Cats sent to scrape the foliage, the never-ending efforts of Devil's Club, slide alder, Indian paintbrush, and Salmonberry bushes. This is a space where everything is feral and weedy, growing and growing, creeping up past the boundaries that separate the regulated and patrolled highway and the wild, wild, western wilderness. Soft shoulder of road, slip of pavement, downward slope from the centre line, a space of refuse and discard.

You are in northern British Columbia. Nowhere most of the world will ever go. A land bordering on the lost. An unseen. A beyond cities, a far outside the imaginings of most.

Still, it is worth looking at. It is worth looking closely at, if only to see what has disappeared, what is missing. Look into the thin shoulder space that borders this highway. Here is what you might find.

Broken beer bottles tossed from cars. Can you hear the hilarity, teenagers partying, driving drunk on unpatrolled roads, sweaty and in love during the few days of heat that summer offers up? Ice-cold beer and the freedom speed of a car, a carburetor-smoking-nearly-used-up-bought-off-a-neighbour car with the windows rolled down and the wind rolling in. Yes, oh yes, toss those beer bottles, watch them shatter, just because you can. Nobody is patrolling you.

Plastic bags, snagged on brambles and translucent as lungs, filled with wind and the rushing exhaust of cars.

Mufflers rotting into metal rust, patterns like muscled lace in thin seepages of water.

Thick black curls of rubber, the ruins of wheels from transport trucks, skid marks like scabs.

Carcasses of broken deer, necks snapped and smears of blood, legs always, always, bent in that running position, some frozen reminder of a futile attempt at escape.

Fallen rocks and the remnants of blasting caps. What is left after dynamite has done its job and the fireweed has come back to ignite the dips and drops; first there are the bright purple flowers, then during pollination the fluffy cotton white. And as it dies, the fireweed gasps into red, a red so red it looks like fresh meat, roadkill.

Things decay and things are consumed in the ditches and crevices on the edge of Highway 16. There are meat and metal and flowers and there is rot and there is rejuvenation. These shoulders are thin and strong, exposed and jutting. Imagine the shoulders of a very young dancer, clavicle bones jutting through flesh. The ever-present risk of breaking.

Broken shoulders.

Soft shoulders and sharp shoulders, such are the shoulders of a sinewy highway, Highway 16.

Things go missing at 120 km per hour on long desolate stretches of road, straight shots between one place that almost no one has heard of and another place even fewer know about. Truck stops and Indian reserves, logging camps and precarious towns clinging to the edges of giant gouges, open pit mines exhaling molybdenum. Endako and Gitsegukla. Kitwanga, Kispiox and New Hazelton. Usk and Rosswood. Smithers and Moricetown.

We have stopped many times on the shoulders of that highway and the time we stopped years ago was not so much different, a detour to the edge.

Pulling off onto the highway's soft shoulder for a soft-shouldered young woman, standing there on the edge of the road on the edge of a town that seems to have no hard and fast boundaries. Smithers simply evaporates. Slowly. From down-town core to mountains, from Main Street to railway track to cabins on lakes to glaciers that trail like tongues up the valleys and into sky.

And the sky is blue the day we stop for her, her in a tight black tank top and tight jeans and jauntiness and confidence on the side of Highway 16, walking backwards on the right shoulder of the road, right hand out, thumb spiked skyward.

By the time we reach Smithers we have already been driving for five hours. We left late but the long summer days make driving all night seem possible. The air is warm. Our car windows are unrolled, our dog is riding in the back seat, head hanging out the window, face streamlined in glee, and we have passed rigs and beehive burners with sparks like fireflies in the long light of late August. We have counted seven black bears, fish-fat fed and glossy handsome, lumbering along the highway's edge. The evening has remained warm but we know it will grow cool before the girl will make it to where she surely must be going. And that is part of the reason we stop. We do not want her to get cold on the edge of the highway.

And of course there is something else.

Moricetown, she says, slipping into the front seat beside me. I'm going to Moricetown.

We have decided I will drive, you will sit in the back seat with our dog, and the girl from the edge of the highway will sit in the front seat beside me. We do not want our dog to make her uncomfortable. So soon she is settled in, all smiles and teeth and chitter-chatter and stories of summer basketball games in Smithers. Stories about kids from the reserves hitching "into town."

Into town, that descriptor that covers every place that is not the reserve, not her reserve with the Moricetown Canyon at its heart, a canyon through which waters boil, waters that men tether themselves over, strapped onto rock faces, spears in hand, the gut-blood of speared salmon spewing into the fine mist that sprays up from the Bulkley River, narrowed for such a breathtakingly short span of space, fish leaping. Salmon by the hundreds for canning and smoking, fillets of red meat crisscrossed and hatched and slung over ladders made of green sapling alder bound with cord and bendable enough to withstand the winds that career in. The wind smells of all of this and more.

And it is precisely this, this smoky-sugared scent of drying fish and the slippery sweat of men tethered to canyon walls, which is everything she wants to escape.

Hitchhiking into town. Because in Smithers the smell of reserve smoke disappears.

How old is she? Fourteen. Going into Grade 9 in the fall. The call of new jeans, runners white and unscuffed, crisp pages of notebooks and moist bright highlighter pens. Geometry sets with not a single missing piece, the protractor's needle perfectly sharp. These are the things she is looking forward to, things she dreams will unfold come the early days of September, come the first whispers of frost.

We curve into Moricetown. Past the roadside hut selling smoked salmon, past the bridge over the canyon, past the Band Office and the community hall and up the hill on the other side of the reserve and onto the shoulder once again. She points out a trail. An almost invisible cleavage in the ditch's vegetation, a path through bush and bramble that we would never have seen had she not known just where to look. We let her out, sunsetting light on her swinging arms as she crosses the highway's shoulder, descends the cupped lip of the ditch and then up the other side and back to her home hidden beyond the tree line.

Our hitchhiker crosses a borderland, walks over the highway's soft shoulder and is lost from our sight. Enveloped by all that grows on the sides of roads.

Soft shoulders disappearing into the evening.

I have picked up other women hitching their way home. Once there was a woman in Gitsegukla, perched on a stack of Coors Light cases, teetering in the dark, hitching back to Kitwanga. I round the curve and my headlights catch her eyes no differently than headlights would catch the eyes of a highway coyote, trotting along the side of the road. Glowing metallic yellow like asteroids. She is so drunk I take her in my arms and fold her into the seat beside me. I pack all the cases of beer into the trunk of my car and I do not argue about the can she keeps in her hand.

She tells me stories as we drive, warm boozy breath wrapping around descriptions of her daughter, her cousins, tales of picking berries or heading down to Vancouver. She is heading home to her auntie's house and in the morning there will be tea. She calls it angel's tea, tea so milky white, warm and sweet, it is like the clouds we see in pictures of heaven. She is certain of this tea, this tea that awaits her. It will mark her return home. And my headlights shine and the ditches on the edge of the highway fade into blackness beyond the light of high beams and her voice hits the pitch of tires on asphalt and we are hurtling together down a mean, mean road.

Think of this highway as a cut. A slice through darkness or wilderness or vegetation or the towns from which we all run.

And now think of this.

A slash right down to the bone can be done in less than three seconds. A slice so deep the skin may never bind, the scar will most assuredly never fade.

Now think of that highway once again and hold your breath and contemplate all the soft shoulders you have touched. Close your eyes and feel the softest slope in the world, the slope at the top of a baby's arm, curve up to neck. The landscape of your lover's clavicle bone, rising and falling with the deep breathing of calm sleep, facing you and the early morning sunlight with a familiarity that knots your stomach and makes you reach out, again and again, just to touch that beautiful skin. Think about every shoulder you have ever touched, ever loved. Think about every person you hold dear.

May you never know what it is to lose your daughter. May you never know a disappearance never explained. A missing without reason or answer or end. May you never dream of your daughter's shoulders buckled and torn in the mud and silt of a ditch. May you never know what mothers know in Moricetown, in Kitwanga, in Burns Lake, Kitwankool, Terrace, Hazelton, Kitimat, Prince Rupert or in Kispiox. May you never think of your daughter as roadside prey.

May you never be the mother of the daughter gone missing from the shoulder of Highway 16 in July, in July when the days can be so cruel. A month of forest fires, a month thick with mosquitoes and decomposition. Fish rot. Of course there are daughters for almost every month of the year because slaughter has no timeline. Thirty-three murdered and missing daughters, sometimes at a rate of more than one per year.

The missing daughter of July was a tree planter. Hitchhiking between Smithers and Prince George, backpack and hemp necklace and a shadow cast on the shoulder of Highway 16. When I think of her I think of long moments when nothing is audible but the sound of wind on the leaves of aspen trees. I think of sun on pavement and the rustle of shrubs and blood red fists of Elderberry thick with juices that birds will drink come fall. I think of the safe stretch of time that existed for her between cars passing. Yes, there would have been that flicker of disappointment when the minivan with a mother and two children did not stop or when that fully loaded logging truck barreled on past. But as long as she was walking, as long as a killer did not stop, that July daughter was safe.

In Moricetown there is a billboard on the side of the highway. "Girls, don't go hitchhiking. Killer on the Loose."

They search for her in waves, ripples of people winding through the ditches. They sift through the foliage and the growth and the rot. Where the roadside slips into fields, they use long sticks and methodically beat back the wheat and alfalfa swaying in the wind. In those roadside tides of green, search crews hope one of them will stumble upon her body. Even a piece of her would be a clue. Please, they think, please let this stick connect with a portion, any broken portion of the family's daughter.

Let her not have gone missing without a trace. Let the soft shoulders of this highway reveal something.

These daughters go missing in the spring and in the winter. They are only occasionally found, frozen and crumpled amongst the roots of alder trees, left torn with pine needles resting on their eyelids, tossed without concern and scratched at by eagles and ravens that draw no distinction between someone's child and the body of a porcupine clipped by a careless driver. Blood on the shoulder of a highway is blood on the shoulder of a highway. So may you never think of your daughter as roadside prey, shoulders soft as dawn, shattered in a ditch overlooked when we travel at highway speeds.

May you never know this truth.

AFTER PAUL AUSTER SPOKE ABOUT LIGHTNING

Film festivals in small northern communities are celebratory.

Sort of.

They give the people who attend them — fleece and toque and handknit socks wearing people of a very particular bent it must be said — a sense of being connected to something afar. Something hard to describe, something urbane, with tall buildings, public transit, and elegant dogs on leashes in parks.

Something the very opposite of sou'westers and mackinaws, cracked mud encrusted leather caulk boots drying beside wood stoves and questions about where to put the septic pond out back and should a bear be shot and how to load the bed of a new twin turbo diesel engine Dodge Ram 4x4 with Arctic Cat snowmobiles.

That is something to celebrate.

Every second year, Terrace hosts a travelling film festival. People in Terrace seem to think the festival is sponsored by the British Columbia Arts Council and the Canada Council for the Arts, both of which speak for themselves in terms of 'being from far away': ask anyone in Terrace and, for sure, no one knows any-one who has ever worked at either of *those* two places.

Posters with lots of white space, sans serif fonts and quirky cute ironic images way too fandangled for most people's tastes get tacked up in the public library, the one restaurant in town that serves vegetarian dishes, the community announcement board above the grocery carts in both of the only two supermarkets, and — down the highway on the Kitsum Kalum Reserve — in the local Band Office.

Someone writes a letter to the editor of the *Terrace Standard* about the waste of taxpayers' money.

The young just-out-of-university high school English teacher develops a special class about censorship, freedom of speech, the arts, and the history of cinematography for her Grade 12 students. That young just-out-of-university high school English teacher is always, always, both brand new every sec-ond year and almost identical to the teacher before her; she moves up north from the city to be close to nature, realizes in the sleety long nights of her first winter that she'd like to have children, dates a trucker a logger a guide outfitter a cop a heavy-duty mechanic a fishermen a heli-ski operator. She tries to explain to him the virtues of lentils and being vegetarian. Then, sometime in mid-August in her second year in the north, a few months after she has broken down and started buying sliced turkey breast at the deli, when the mosquitoes just stop being too bad to even walk outside and you can finally read a book on the back deck of the trailer on the back forty which is one of the few homes for rent near town, she moves back down south after attending the film festival, during which she cries while sitting alone in the theatre's back row.

If you try to stifle your sobs at one of the movies during the every-second-year film festival, by leaning your head back while seated in the last row of seats in Terrace's movie theatre, which is an independent venture in case you didn't know, run by a husband and wife team who also own a logging camp up in Nisga'a Territory and an RV sales park on the edge of town and who have done pretty well for themselves over the last thirty-five years, the back of your head will touch gold shag carpets that run up, down, and all around the walls of the Tillicum Twin Theatres.

The logo of the theatres, by the way, is a Thunderbird totem pole carved by Mungo Martin in Victoria, which looks out across the Pacific Ocean 1445.5 kilometres southwest of Terrace. No one thinks this is unusual or says anything about it in Terrace because no one pays any attention to things like Thunderbirds who beat their massive wings, splitting open storm-silver skies with sheet lightning flashing from their eyes, from whom humans descended all those millions and millions of years ago when there was nothing but night and the earth was purely stone.

The shag carpets were Bill and Norma's mid-1980s' effort at soundproofing, golden fleece that is now crispy and disintegrating to the touch.

Bill and Norma's soundproofing idea means that after leaving the films that made you cry, made you dream of Ethiopian food restaurants and bookstores with Friday evening poetry readings, you have to pick bits of carpet scab from your scalp.

If you dared to put some kind of fancy hair product in your hair, let's say a nice smelling wax or sculpting gel because you dared to dream that you might meet another young teacher who might want to walk along a northern river hand in hand with you and then go home with you and make a salad with homegrown bean sprouts, the bits of gold carpet will stick to your hair, the back and top of your head, for days.

Even after a good washing, several days later you will find golden carpet scales on your pillow one morning when you wake up alone and exhausted by the size of everything around you. You might remember your fright when the rivers began to flood full-throttle, tearing out whole cottonwood trees, because it seemed like those rivers were out to destroy the world.

Dolby Sound has yet to arrive in Terrace and who needs 3-D anyway because most of those films come in the format we've been fine with for the last ten years. If Bill and Norma are going to change things up at the Tillicum Twin Theatres, they'd be better off getting rid of the bank of urinals in the women's washroom that no one, and I mean no one, has ever been able to explain. After all, it's not like there aren't urinals in the men's washroom too, which, OK yes, aren't exactly aligned and could be better affixed to the wall, which everyone knows about because at least one guy someone knows has had a hard time aiming, and even missed when the kids in the race-car-driving video machines leaning against the other side of the urinal wall got really mad about not being able to go faster in their video race cars and kick-slammed the machines, hard, causing the urinals to shudder.

Still, even with the gold shag carpet and the race-car shuddering urinals, one weekend every twenty-four months at the Tillicum Twin Theatres in Terrace is taken up by Montreal documentaries, experimental shorts, indie flicks about snow boarders and skaters around Vancouver, films by Iranian feminists and, in the case of a film I saw when I was seventeen and recall particularly well, a slow-moving drama with unflattering sequences of a very thin woman in her mid-sixties, fading blue shoulder blade butterfly tattoo, mounting a young man's erect cock in his university dorm.

In Terrace, the forty or so people who attend the film festival, many of them Grade 12 students revved up about freedom of speech and thinking about university even though their parents tell them it is not worth the price of admission and it's a helluvalot smarter to meet the foreman of CN Rail or the manager at the local sawmill, all experience these movies together. We all lean forward together. For the sixteen or so hours of a dust-specked flickering funnel of light and the snap-snap-snap of reels ending, those of us watching the eight films that arrived by bus from Prince Rupert and are sometimes late because of mud and debris slides, hold our breath. Together. And exhale. Together.

Together for the hours of those films we give up the long strong light of late summer evenings that sustains us in the winter and we give up the first runs of coho and the possibility of picking pine mushrooms and we give up the most purple of purples in the world, in the shape of fireweed flowers before they turn to seed and pollen, ash white on the wind bringing in fall, and we are transported, connected to something afar.

It is much the same in Prince George.

Yes, Prince George is 573 kilometres east of Terrace along Highway 16 and, yes, Prince George has a film festival not every second year but instead for three full days every single winter and then one alternative film is screened at the local college every week during the autumn. Yes, in that way Prince George is far away from Terrace: It's a city with a Costco and a Winners and more than one high school and a university and a movie theatre with six screens, all of which play digital and have 3-D options.

Still, Prince George is a northern city, a city circled by gravel logging roads punched through wilderness fast and hard to make way for clear-cutting and hauling away the dead wood from millions of hectors of pine-beetle-killed-forests. It is a city chockablock full of women who, in the winter when it is -30 or sometimes colder, are forced to go to work in skirts and fake fur-lined rubber boots because otherwise their feet would freeze when they shovel the driveway in the morning, their husbands away in camp or out on a rig somewhere, hands winter chapped and sometimes even bleeding from grabbing chains slick with bitumen or natural gas.

The same year that a Canadian film was nominated for an Oscar, which was a big deal even though Canadians were bitter that the nomination was in the category of Best Foreign Language Film, which seemed crazy to most of us who live in bilingual Canada but speak only English and who for the most part live within two hundred kilometres of the United States border, the film festival in Prince George screened a documentary about people struck by lightning.

Act of God is a quiet film, at odds with the topic it contemplates. A group of mothers stand on the yellow-red ground of a small desert village in Mexico and look toward the moon, toward the stars, forgiving the sky for having released an evening lightning bolt that sizzled down along a metal rooftop cross and through the adobe ceiling of their town's tiny church, killing a number of their children.

The New York City author Paul Auster, whose books are among my all-time favorites and whose thin text *Why Write*, with a lightning bolt slashed across its cover, is one I have returned to hundreds of times for clarity on a question that often plagues me, speaks very softly in the film about a night that changed his life forever.

On a summer evening in 1961, Paul Auster and a group of fellow early-teen boys at a summer camp in rural New York State were led off by a group counselor eager to expose the city boys to some real and authentic nature. In 1961, Paul Auster was of course still very young and so was very different from the man in the film who (so I had read) by then had a son who'd gone to prison and who had taken up writing novels about improbable things like doing nothing but moving stones for years on end. In the story in the movie *Act of God* that Paul Auster narrates, the cluster of boys began walking through rolling farmers' fields toward a thin line of forest on the horizon. Clouds above the boys boiled and the light slowly transformed into that awful bruised tint of pewter that people for the most part know means that a storm is getting ready, really good and ready.

In the movie, Paul Auster tells the story of that night slowly and matter-of-factly.

It begins to rain.

The boys are soaked.

The storm begins in earnest.

The sky is full of sheet lightning.

The lightning is splintering blinding blue terrible and everywhere.

The boys turn around and head back for camp, confused with the fury of the world unleashed all around them. They come across a fence they don't remember crossing earlier. They form a line and one boy hoists up the bottom line of barbwire so the other boys, slick with mud and rain by now, can shimmy under. All the boys make it under and then it's the turn of the last boy, the one who held the barbwire up for everyone else, including Paul Auster.

As the last boy begins to gingerly slide under the fence, a bolt of lightning reaches down and electrifies the fence, lighting up the metal into thin sparking bands of vibrating blue heat.

I remember how quietly Paul Auster spoke about that bolt of lightning. How measured he appeared when he spoke about the bolt of lightning that shot down and through his friend, killing the boy instantly.

I think about lightning being a reason to write.

When I leave the Prince George theatre where the three-day movie festival is always screened, the night is bright and calm. There is not even an idea of lightning. Fresh snow has fallen sometime during a film earlier in the day. The moon, while not quite a complete orb, is certainly big, a sliver or two off full. Stars sparkle and my boots squeak on the icy pavement as I walk toward my car. Still, visions of lightning shoot through my eyes when I close them, inhaling the cold winter air. I can still hear Paul Auster's voice in my head. I get into my car and pull out of the parking lot and I make a right-hand turn onto the highway that runs past one of Prince George's many grocery stores and I think about how I still live close to nature but also in a big city, comparatively speaking, and I think about movie festivals that I attended when I was much, much younger, and I then for a moment I think about Terrace.

I remember clearly this is what I was thinking about because, the very second that I think about Terrace, a pearly white Cadillac SUV streaks past me, a flash of white going at least triple my speed. I watch its bright speeding tail lights rush towards a four-way intersection just up ahead, an intersection where I'd subconsciously noted the lights just turning red. The Cadillac does not stop. It plows front first into a small Toyota, the same year and make as the Toyota I am driving home from a documentary film while thinking about lightning and think-ing about the theatre in Terrace.

I am the first person to arrive at the intersection. The small Toyota, crumpled on impact and spun several times around in the intersection before smashing into a power pole on the edge of the highway, is steaming. Steaming. All around, glass sparkles on the ice and snow that dust the highway. Despite smashing into another car, the SUV has made it well through the intersection and has stopped several metres past the traffic lights, the traffic lights that are still going through their yellow-red-green sequence, oblivious to the carnage below them. I stop in the middle of the intersection under those lights, jump out of my car and run towards the driver's side of the struck car.

Lights are popping behind my eyes, a combination of shock and seeing bright sparks that lit up the night when metal chewed into and skidded against other metal. As I reach the crumpled car, a young woman with long blonde hair struggles to get out of the driver's seat, her feet crunching on glass. I hear a dog barking, a sharp high-pitched abnormal yipping as brittle as the light on glass on ice on the pavement. The woman slips, stumbling for a split second. I try to catch her while at the same time reaching to open the passenger's door behind the driver's seat. A white plastic baby car seat is buckled down in the back seat. A box of Cheerios has exploded, little "Os" littering surfaces of slowly deflating airbags. A carton of milk is ripped open, pouring over a head of lettuce that landed behind the front passenger seat. Nothing is moving in the baby seat, a pastel flowered flannel blanket tucked snuggly in around the shape of a tiny human, face invisible, everything quiet save for the bark of a dog I now see is in the far back of the car.

For a moment I have no idea what to do.

The young woman is calling from behind me 'is she OK is she OK is she OK' and the question seems in perfect rhythm with the bark of the dog and the turning of the traffic lights and the sputtering steam of the car and my breath and my heart and my breath again and I am bending into the car unbuckling the baby seat, gently maneuvering out a plastic bucket that is shaped like a cupped hand. As I turn away from the shadow of the wrecked car, light settles upon the flannel blanket and everything is glinting inside the baby seat, shards of glass coating the pink flowered flannel blanket, resting on silence. I set the baby seat on the pavement and in the distance I hear sirens and the woman is still calling is she OK is she OK is she ok is she ok, this time closer, right next to me, beside me, and I see my hands and I see the hands of the mother and we are reaching into the white plastic cupped hand and slowly peeling back the flannel blanket, the sound of bits of glass dropping onto ice on pavement and then there is the face of a baby.

And then that baby screams.

Oh she screams.

The dog stops barking.

The young woman is sobbing, sobbing, gingerly lifting the baby from the car seat, crouching with baby pressed into chest and then sitting on the edge of the highway median beside her steaming car.

I walk around to the back of the car and open the hatchback and I take the dog by his collar and I lead him to his owner and then we are all sitting. The dog is shaking. Shuddering really. His whole body. I hold onto his collar with my left hand and with my right hand I rub the woman's back, circles circles circles as the sirens approach, bright blue lights. The baby is still screaming. I look at my feet and notice a smear of coagulating blood on the toe of my boot. I have no idea where it came from. I have not noticed any bleeding. I think about cameras, panning slowly, shooting all the films I have seen in my life. I recall walking out of a darkened theatre into a darkening summer evening when I was a teenager in Terrace, the stationary outstretched wings of a Thunderbird above me, somewhere a storm, somewhere a northern river in summer flood, the winter snowpack melting far away in mountain valleys I have still not seen.

AESOP

Take off your undershirt, sweat-stained from almost four hours of snowshoeing along the Skeena River. Take off your threadbare Stanfields, wet and salty.

That, says my dad, is the kind of scent strong enough to draw back a dog.

If there is any food in the truck, even an apple core or a previously melted and then congealed Mars bar from last summer, leave that too. Despite the likelihood (no, more like the almost certainty) that a winter-starved coyote or fox will eat it before the dog shows up, it is a good idea to leave it anyway.

Wrap the shirt tightly around some leafless shrub, something at least a few feet above the snow line. So even if there is a blizzard, the thick smell of your skin won't be engulfed, won't be claimed by another snowbank. Will, instead, hover and call out to a dog.

My dad wanted Aesop to return.

My dad chose a red osier dogwood to tie his undershirt around.

For just under a minute, in the -27 degree evening, around 4:50 p.m. when he knew he was already late for dinner, my father pulled off his coat, his sweater, his orange flannel button-up shirt and then his Stanfields undershirt and he stood bare-chested in a northern British Columbia winter. Imagine this. Imagine that everything was dark, that the islands of cottonwoods tucking into loamy soils of eskers were invisible in night and snow and that even the scent of decomposing autumn leaves was frozen inert and lost under the weight of a sky that let loose metres and metres of snow.

My dad wrapped his shirt around the shrub. He dressed again, in the cold, and his flannel shirt would have stuck to his skin.

He hoped Aesop would catch the undershirt's scent and return to it and wait until my father came back later that night, around midnight, and again the next morning before sunrise and then again that evening. And the following morning. And the night after that.

In the winter, dogs chase down moose.

In the winter, moose run down railway tracks, gunnels of snowless trails, easy straight lines walled by metres of snow but clear themselves.

Moose never outrun trains. Caught in the headlights, they litter railway tracks as sprayed carcasses. Hundreds are killed every year.

My parents plucked Aesop off the side of the highway when they were driving north to Tuktoyaktuk with plans to fly onto Herschel Island, a permafrosted dot thick with whalebones that have washed ashore for hundreds and hundreds of years. The flight path to Herschel Island took my parents over the Mackenzie River Delta, so big it was hard to tell where river ended and the Arctic Ocean began.

Endless, my dad recalls, endless.

Aesop was sitting on the side of the Dempster Highway. He shat caterpillars and moths for weeks, a shit-stream of what he'd been living on before my dad grabbed him by the scruff of the neck and chucked him in the back of their Toyota, up on top of the cooler, a stack of sleeping bags, and the two tents my mum and dad always camp with.

The dog was, my dad said, stupider than the sticks he never tired of chasing when my dad went out fishing with him.

Just before my dad returned that evening, snowshoeing again into the cold and luminescent snow, this time with a new and warm undershirt on, he said simply, "I hope that fucking dog wasn't stupid enough to try and run down a moose on the railway tracks." After that, he went out looking again and again and again, the next morning, the afternoon after that, and then for many more evenings in the following weeks. Only a dog would know if the scent of my father's undershirt faded with time.

COLUMBUS BURNING

i

From the sky are falling ashes the size of opened hands, fingers splayed, palms facing upwards. Unsteady.

More precisely, the ashes are the size of the open hands of a big and broken man, toque fallen before him, standing on a grey sidewalk in the bruised orange and grey hue of a fire that is busting the sky wide open. Whoosh, whoosh, whoosh. Oxygen vanishing. The scream of fire trucks. Soon water will rain down on those flames, those flames the man feels hot on his face.

He is watching his bed burning. He is watching his single occupancy room vanish in a hotel fire. Painted letters, stencilled across a façade, sizzle. The Columbus Hotel, Built In 1920, is being consumed.

And the water will be too late and the night will have been too long.

The hotel's namesake landed far away from this fire, in a different lifetime. And anyway, this man is not interested in histories from books or from people who do nothing but talk. Their words are not the words of people for whom he cares or who care for him.

Still, if someone asked him, and if that someone waited patiently for an answer, the man might very quietly recite something that stirs his memory of school days: "In fourteen hundred ninety-two, Columbus sailed the ocean blue. He had three ships and left from Spain, He sailed through sunshine, wind, and rain. He sailed by night; he sailed by day. He used the stars to find his way."

Today there is no wayfinding to be had because home has vanished. All orientations to important and intimate things are going up in flames.

So this man knows a different Columbus. A Columbus burning.

ii

My foot connects with an ash. A flake of charred roofing material drifting down the sidewalk in downtown Prince George. I am walking past the husk of what last week was a building but is now a gaping hole with jagged edges, walls collapsing inward, sky visible through the roof, the corner of a bed's wrought iron headboard resting against a window frame. The road is cordoned off, police still moving about. Bright red bags, strips of reflector ribbon, yellow tape, emergency equipment, and cameras.

One block away is the local farmers' market. Today I have a grocery list that includes fresh salsa, bread, basil, honey, and eggs. In the distance is a siren, but it is far away.

This is a city that guidebooks warn tourists and travellers away from. Prince George, the guidebooks tell tourists, is not a place to linger. When you go north, say the guidebooks, look for pristine wilderness. When you have witnessed such primitive purity, your metropolises become all the more civilized by comparison. Think of yourself as an early explorer. Look for vast unsullied tracts of ancient rain forest, glaciers and mountain ranges, the lumbering bodies of grizzly bears.

Do not linger amongst the railway yards and boxcars. Do not linger amongst the potholes and rusted-out pickup trucks. Do not linger in parks that lay no claim to manicured beauty or beside river banks upon which the carcasses of fish rot, soft flesh red and torn, the high-pitched whistle of eagles touching down as cycles older than time unfold, cycles of death and decay. Do not linger in a town where, in the middle of winter at minus forty, ice jams up in the veins of rivers, groaning like monstrous mating animals, flooding out residents and confirming a state of unluckiness.

Do not linger in Prince George, a city with a worn-out downtown core through which trawl worn-out whores, a city that grabs national media attention only when a Supreme Court judge admits to raping and assaulting young First Nations sex-trade workers, children trying to survive long after Christopher Columbus's men were serviced by girls they transformed into vectors, veins filled with the blood of Spain.

iii

Does the man with open hands, palms facing upward, know anything about the blood of Spain? He has no interest. He does, though, know a thing or two about girls trying to survive on the streets of Prince George.

He knows all he needs to know about Columbus because he lived in the Columbus Hotel.

In downtown Prince George.

Above the bar and strip club.

Before this fire he entered his home, the hotel, through the front of the building, past a small sign reading "Live Girls and Home Cooked Meals." He entered under green awnings, wilted from the weight of snow fallen over too many winters to count. Then up the staircase to the hallway that led to his room. The corridor had flimsy doors on either side, indents in the wood, yellow lighting, sweaty warmth and the soft thudding of music downstairs, the smell of going on one hundred years of old beer sloshed on a long bar counter that decades ago lost any sign of lustre or shine. The door to his room does not have a number yet he knows his door with all his heart.

If you pressed the man about Christopher Columbus, he might call forth a few more lines from that children's rhyme: "A compass also helped him know, How to find the way to go. Ninety sailors were on board; Some men worked while others snored. Then the workers went to sleep; And others watched the ocean deep." He might laugh at this, thinking of the thin walls in the Columbus Hotel. How he can hear men snoring. How commercial fishermen masquerading as sailors are sometimes stranded in the bar downstairs, far away from the coastline, watching the girls, wanting the ocean.

He has passed hundreds of girls in the hallway of the place he calls home. He has watched them fighting men and fighting back tears. He has fought back tears himself, sitting late at night on the edge of his bed, surrounded by the four walls that contain his entire life.

Remember that this man was once a boy and a brother and once, in what feels like another lifetime in a place as far away as the coast upon which Christopher Columbus first set foot, this man was a father.

But now this is his home. He lives here with ten other people who live in ten other single occupancy rooms. Each room is the home, yes home, of its occupant. It is a place of memory and occasional desire. A place of moments between sleep and wakefulness, of minutes first thing in the morning when dreams have not yet evaporated and the light is just breaking and we are utterly alone in the world with no one but ourselves.

The fire begins at 6:30 in the morning. No alarms sound. No sprinkler system automatically starts up. A century of dry wood is like kindling, slivers so perfect for burning there is almost no sound, just an instant and quiet inferno.

iv

On that August morning I awake to the sound of cottonwood leaves jostling, crows calling and dogs barking in the opening hours of what will be a warm summer day of long light. A thin smell of smoke that I do not give much thought to. I have not yet learned of the fire.

So I linger. In my home. In a city that is my home because I have a home to call my own within it. I linger in my many rooms, and I look out over the Mountain Ash trees in my back-yard and a greenhouse full of tomato plants and an alleyway that is shaded with lilac bushes and is part of system of alley-ways that Prince George residents take pride in and visitors are surprised by and tourists never see. I linger with thoughts of walking along the Fraser River, the Nechako River, two of the mightiest rivers in all of Canada. I linger over a cup of coffee and as I linger I turn on the radio and I hear the news.

A blaze in the Columbus Hotel.

Columbus burning.

Reporters refer to it as a blaze. Like the name of a stallion, like a radiant flash. Like a rage.

That raging brightness has eaten one man alive, firefight-ers plucking him from the blaze, ambulances screaming him towards the hospital that he does not arrive at alive. I imagine a trail of searing pain. I imagine the small stings of hurt left after my arm touched the edge of an iron or my palm accidently slipped onto a pan just pulled from the oven.

I imagine this under every inch of my skin, a burning throughout every capillary, a cloak of fire. I do not want to die this way. I want no one to die this way.

The smoke hanging in the air contains fragments of a man who has burned to death. In everything I smell, I am breathing him in.

Two other men are missing amongst the ashes and cinders and rubble.

And then I hear the voices of people interviewed about the blaze, an occasional siren sounding behind them, sure signs they are standing close to the still hot ground where the Columbus Hotel was, just hours before, the home of men.

The voice of a woman: "It's about time. It should have happened years ago. There's no place here for places like that."

The voice of another woman: "It's a tragedy. A real tragedy. I just can't believe it."

The voice of a man: "This city should clean places like that up. This kind of thing should never have happened."

Then there are written words, notes left in the placeless places of blogs and internet chat rooms: "I think we should burn the whole thing down and start over. The downtown is ugly and there is no reason for law-abiding citizens to be there past 8:00 p.m. Prince George needs to be purged."

And: "It is with great sadness that we have to say goodbye to another historical building here in Prince George. It may not have been a place where I chose to spend my time. But it was a part of Prince George. My heart goes out to those involved in this horrible event, those who have lost all their cherished belongings and homes and possibly their lives as well."

I am lingering. Listening. In my home in a city where Columbus burned. Slowly the scent of lilac flowers will chase away the smell of smoke.

v

The man is big because he carries the immense weight of all his life inside the contours of his skin, clinging to his bones. He is made of memories and moments and losses so great that he will never speak of them and in silence they grow, expanding so that no space is large enough to contain them. And so he chose a tiny place to enclose his great pains. Perhaps within the tight parameters of a single occupancy room the hauntings will simply grow weary, exhaust themselves, and disappear.

He hoped this every day. Every day he spread open his hands, looked down upon his wide palms, and hoped the burning pain inside him would subside. He searched for this, like those men in the children's rhyme: "Day after day they looked for land; They dreamed of trees and rocks and sand. October 12 their dream came true, You never saw a happier crew! 'Indians! Indians!' Columbus cried; His heart was filled with joyful pride."

On August 19th all the man's dreams vanish.

His search for land and trees and rocks that made up fleeting moments of a childhood, which he held deep inside him like a dark warm stone and about which he inexplicably daydreamed and allowed himself some sense of hope, all vanish.

And he knows this and he knows something else. Something just as mean as flames. It is a something left unsaid all around him, flitting just outside the boundaries of what is acceptable to utter aloud.

But he knows it is there. Indians! Indians! in the rooms of the Columbus Hotel: "Columbus sailed on to find some gold To bring back home, as he'd been told. He made the trip again and again, Trading gold to bring to Spain."

Gold has never crossed the palms of the men who live in the Columbus Hotel. The trips they made, again and again and again, were between their rooms and the street. Now they have no rooms between them and the street.

The cause of the fire is a clothes dryer. A faulty wire. Early in the morning a nameless occupant in a numberless room above a bar and strip club was doing his weekly washing. Taking damp laundry from the washing machine, perhaps shaking out each item (a towel, a pair of pants, two socks, and a pillow case) and tossing them into the drum of a dryer. This should not kill people. This should not leave people homeless.

Days later the bodies of the two missing men are pulled from the rubble.

The man is not there to witness this. He is wandering the streets in a city that wants to purge him.

He no longer has a place to linger. But he is not whom the guidebooks were written for. He is not whom the history books were written for. He was the occupant of Columbus burning.

CHARTING THE FINITE

Space is infinite between the needle's eye and the moistened thread tip held carefully by my Oma's thumb and index finger. It is the space of lifetimes, measured in landscapes as wide as the west coast of Vancouver Island during smelt season, in places tiny as pores on a thimble.

To remember you is to place you, memory mapping, place becoming experience becoming you; although you are lost (people are sorry for my loss) I am still with you, emplaced. I am with you through landscapes I have seen and never seen, the landscapes of your home, a strange feeling you once explained to me, a feeling of the heart slowing, a painful tightening of throat, cheeks, and muscles between mandibles, almost crying with the joy of returning simultaneous with the relief that you left these great flatlands of green and tulips below sea level, an impossibility, a deep sadness that a new home will always be new, will always be a translation of mother tongue into learned language.

Let me chart you through the finite.

I know such smallness does not do justice to eighty-seven years lived. I know the gaps are immense. But allow me to conjure you nevertheless and between us we can inhabit places among the lost.

Nothing remains of the first place I recall: 120 1st Street in Duncan, British Columbia, the first house you owned in Canada, the first house in which my father introduced you to my mother, the house where I first learned Dutch was an immigrants' language which would be spoken around me, never to me.

Homescape.

A front yard with carefully tended flower beds, a white picket fence, a concrete path from sidewalk to front door: This was the door used by women you sewed for, never by family. Husband, children, grandchildren, we all used the side door, at the end of the driveway running parallel to the parking lot of a mechanic's cinderblock shop, we maneuvered past parked cars, past window boxes, feet crunching on gravel, then through the screen door set in fibreglass yellowed with age. Looking back I know it must have looked like a house tended by the Dutch. A small soft yellow house made of clapboard and surrounded by industrial parking lot, Credit Union, the edges of small businesses, coffee shops, furniture warehouses, and stores growing up in a rural town quickly urbanizing. Starched white curtains hung in every window, always pulled, a reflection of the Netherlands where all windows looked into the windows of others.

Behind those curtains were sites of wonder.

The women you sewed for entered the front door and turned left, through my father's and uncle's bedroom that even during their school years had to be tidied each morning so as to appear uninhabited, empty. The women were Canadian, looking for a European seamstress; they stood in this stark bedroom for fittings, walked the short distance from bedroom to living room (across a hall carpeted in wool you hooked over so many hundreds of evenings) in order to look at themselves in a mirror hanging beside one of the single items of furniture you'd transported from the Netherlands. A mirror, with leaded flowers edging the perimeter, hanging beside a chest of drawers with large brass handles. Sometimes my sister and I would watch those women turn spin turn, your hands like birds, smoothing down, pinning, fussing, always complementary. Then we would return to the sewing room, your *atelier*, with the plywood table where your sewing machine arched above us from our seats on the floor, surrounded by fabric scraps, mohair and raw silk, things better than I knew I would ever wear, and we would listen to your tales of Nazis chasing Opa down Schiedam's narrow streets, of great Opa Bart throwing ceramic bassinets from third story windows in order to distract young fascist soldiers while Jews were hustled in the opposite direction.

Beneath that plywood sewing table, Husqvarna machine knock knock knocking needle and thread through fabric, I learned of your childhood swimming, your father the lemonade factory owner, your young womanhood as a costumier, the small shop you ran and the exquisite *haute couture* of gowns and costumes for all of Swan Lake. I travelled through your memories of war, of you folding family garnets into the diapers of your first tiny daughter, breast-feeding so that your own teeth blackened with a lack of nutrition, soldiers at your door, bombs as you stitched, Dutch women with heads shaved bald led down main streets, their sin that of sleeping with Nazis, and still today I am haunted by young women's faces, thin with eyes wide and full of pain, no hair to frame the bone, to soften the hurt.

Canada must have smiled in your imagination. Promises were gifted to you through Opa and down to your three children, the landscape a dream. We now know the story, but then it was real enough for a banner to be stitched, gecko sprawling across orange flag fabric, our surname intertwined with the business my Opa was promised, a man who up until the move to Canada had made his living as a musician, a man transforming himself into an entrepreneur, operator and co-owner of an exotic animal zoo in Duncan, British Columbia.

Surely you must have sensed oddness. Did you not wonder aloud about the prospects of a zoo on the west coast of Canada?

Of course this was before the time of television and computers and access to information anywhere and everywhere. You had read about Canada, about the vast wilderness dotted with small towns and young cities. Reading about place, though, differs greatly from accurately imagining place. Everything you imagined was in reference to the known. and you had never known the likes of a small town on Vancouver Island. You had travelled, were well travelled in places from Yugoslavia to Britain. You must have had some confidence about the unknown, but what must have happened to that confidence when you set foot in that first house, years before you would own 120 1ˢᵗ Street?

Even now, more than forty years since you unpacked everything you did not have, after you catalogued everything you renounced for the move to Canada, that first house is a painfully small mark in an open countryside, nothing but rolling fields into mountains and sky. Easily ten kilometres outside of Duncan, the closest town, with fewer than 5,000 people. And you were not alone. That four room farm house was shared with the family who brought you here, the family to whom your husband paid money for a business partnership, dreams of iguanas and porpoises so comical once you had your family in place: four rooms for nine people, so terribly claustrophobic within a landscape so open that you may have for the first time contemplated endlessness. The collision of such opposites sets the stage for your life in Canada. Years later you tell me your heart was always divided between two landscapes.

It is not without pain that a heart remains divided.

I grow up with the stories of that pain. Pain of leaving your family and mother tongue, of traversing first the great grayness of the Atlantic Ocean, of travelling by train across the massive landscape of Canada, of arriving on the west coast, on an island as large as your entire home country. Over the years I came to know that pain is the reason behind so many of your stories, stories about these Canadians who know nothing about culture and sophistication, stories about landscapes devoid of art or high fashion, stories always in part anchored in the landscape that, although left behind, continued to haunt your every glance and expectation.

You leave that tiny shared farmhouse and move into the downtown of Duncan, an alligator, several iguanas, and a tortoise in tow as the remnants of Opa's zoo, which travel with you to the small plot of green grass behind your new home. Opa is despondent, filled with resentment toward most everything he encounters. He insists Canadians know nothing about music and for months he suffers a terrible migraine, finally insisting that he must return to Holland. He gives you no indication that he will ever come back to Canada and you begin your livelihood of sewing, caring for your three children while barely able to speak English. When you tell me this story, you begin it at the end; Opa returning following months of silence, the pressure in his head released after a Dutch doctor inserted a sliver spike into his sinus cavity, a single quick thrust breaking bone which had grown over membrane. The release of pressure does nothing to lessen his disdain for Canada. His long trip back to the Netherlands confirms for him the great inadequacies of Canada with which he is forced to cope. It makes no impression on Opa that you are trying to form a community, inviting other Dutch immigrants over to your house, joining local theatre groups so that years later we discover newspaper clippings, yellowed with age, which depict you smiling and holding trophies won with fellow members of the Cowichan Valley Community Theatre Group.

For almost two decades you work at creating a homescape in this new landscape of Canada. Your children finish elementary school, junior and senior high school; they graduate and go on to universities and although Opa does not work you think of him as contributing to the household. Your home is full of crows rescued by Opa; they perch on branches secured to bookcases, looking down with missing eyes and broken wings upon the ever growing alligator and tortoise who roam freely through the house. At different times roosters inhabit the house, iguanas in windowsills, kittens sprawling across the alligator's back as they all warm themselves in front of woodstoves which Opa tends, cutting kindling thinly and precisely. Still, it is not until your eldest son gets a job at the local pulp mill, securing a seasonal job which opens eligibility for a mortgage that the work of a seamstress did not, that you are finally able to move into a house you can call your own. Slowly, in the early mornings and late evenings that are balanced around fittings and hours of sewing, you begin to mend the split in your heart by tending a tiny landscape in homage to the country you left behind.

A greenhouse is built to house your orchids, wide-mouthed flowers in garish colours and tiger stripes, lips splayed to reveal bright tongues. Opa constructs baskets of small cedar slats nailed carefully together like intertwined fingers. He ensures sphagnum moss is always plentiful, stuffed to overflowing into the baskets and then hanging them from the greenhouse rafters to allow space for the long white orchids roots to hang down. He builds fans to circulate the moisture produced by a complex spray system he rigs up, he fiddles with the oil stove he's fit into the corner of the greenhouse. This greenhouse, taking up almost half the backyard at 120 1st Street, is full of a thick tropical smell, wet and musty, floral and green simultaneously. You display your orchids proudly, as if their flowery royalty erases the fact that your fingers are now bent from years of seamstress work, as if their beautiful mouths sing so loudly as to quiet your Dutch accent, your transition to English. You are vain through your flowers, vain in this landscape which tried to render you subservient.

You plant gardens all around the tiny house that calls out Dutchness. In the summer the house wafts perfumes which overpower the car exhaust around a home increasingly encroached upon by urban growth. Flower boxes overflow with petunias. Broad beans and lima beans (to be stewed and served with mint sauce, cabbage, potatoes, and tough cuts of meat fried slowly in margarine) climb lattices nailed together by Opa, dragon snaps, hyacinths, and nicotiana all stand carefully aligned in front of an always freshly painted white picket fence. Opa finally finds work as a street cleaner for the municipality. Something close to settledness descends upon the small yellow house. In the summer the alligator pushes through the knee-high fence around a side garden under the kitchen window, doggedly marching on the squat legs which move his now six foot long body. Aquariums are filled with the fat and languid orange bodies of carp and goldfish. There is finally a seasonal certainty which you struggled to attain when you first left the Netherlands.

In the winter your greenhouse steams against Canada's ice and cold, snow slipping off the heated glass roof. Christmas brings home your children and now grandchildren; you bake Dutch treats of fried bread filled with raisins and apple bits, sprinkling icing on the cold fritters laid out on sheets of newspaper in the bedroom just next to your atelier. Spring thaws soil, turned by hand for planting, an ever-present resistance to the parking lots which now touch all three sides of your little plot of green. In summer you travel to the west coast of Vancouver Island, your children now adults and their children too becoming adults, all of us running along the sand beaches of Port Renfrew, setting the long nets perpendicular to the waves, waiting to haul in catches of brilliantly silver smelt. These fish will always remind you of herring in Holland, eaten raw with coarse salt. So much of your new life still harkens back to a landscape left behind, but slowly the split in your heart is closing. In the fall you fill freezer bags with fruits, let walnuts dry on every flat surface available inside the house. African violets, a purple so deep it almost resembles blood, slowly whither on your kitchen counter, and you write yourself notes, sitting in the chair at the end of the table looking over your home, notes about the number of orchids you need to re-pot, about the loaves of bread required for the next week, the rounds of gouda which should be bought, the skirts which need to be adjusted or hemmed.

This home is your new country, a landscape created anew. You left a homeland and created a land of home. This homescape is everything I remember you by. The small places etched into my memory are what I recall you by. In total over thirty years passed in a tiny house standing defiantly against pavement, parking lot, road, furniture stores, and banks. It is in my memory of place that you live, seated in the evening, after tying up your hair, on the couch under vines of Hoya plants, needlepoint spread over your lap, silver thimble protecting your fingertip, thread held between thumb and index finger, an infinity, a full full life.

THIS IS SUNDAY MORNING, COMIN' DOWN

Saturday night, standing on my back porch. The evening after the last finger of snow has finally melted from under the eaves of the greenhouse.

You tell me about your dream of coyotes.

The late spring evening is folding up and turning dark and you're getting ready to head home after your final cigarette before tomorrow and there's a Johnny Cash song playing on the radio. We can hear it coming through the kitchen window: *'Cause there's something in a Sunday that makes a body feel alone. And there's nothing short a' dying, that's half as lonesome as the sound of the sleeping city sidewalk, and Sunday morning coming down.*

You take the last pull on your cigarette, flick the remains across the lawn and the sky turns a darker blue. *Sunday morning coming down.*

Tomorrow will be a morning of loneliness that nothing short of death can eclipse. I will awake and, in a tiny flicker between sleep and a new day, the image of a friend will appear. For the briefest part of a second I will feel the world as a split world, as if she were not dead. Then it will dawn. A new day. On me. She is dead and her dying is short of nothing.

Her dying will be upon me, as it is every Sunday morning, splitting the world.

For a while you haven't said anything, watching the bluing evening bring Saturday to a close. Then you tell me coyotes visited you twice in the last two days. On the Thursday and Friday before you are talking to me.

First, on Thursday, you were speaking with your oldest son, telling him about different ways of seeing the world. Your son is all busted up and confused, you say. He's losing a business he tried to start about two years ago because he ignored practical advice about ways to keep the accounts, about needing to pay his taxes on time. His latest girlfriend's also just left him, because he didn't ever listen to her perspectives either.

When he tells you all of this you suddenly decide, for no reason at all that you can think of, to tell him the story you were told many years ago about Coyote. About Coyote who didn't heed the words of Rabbit, who it should be noted was a very wise being with many powerful talents, who warned him about greed and overuse of rare gifts. In the Coyote story you were told, which is along the same lines as the Coyote story told to many other children who lived near you when you were all growing up in that shitty one-horse town split down the middle between Indians and not-Indians in rolling fields of southern Alberta, Coyote was out strolling the world one morning when he saw Rabbit do a most incredible thing.

Rabbit was taking his eyes out of their sockets and sending them off on their own to see many different things, making sure there weren't any dangers up ahead, being sure around the next corner there was enough grass to have a full belly through the winter. Up to the sky went Rabbit's eyes, having a close look at feathers on a hawk. Down into the ground went Rabbit's eyes, having an up-close gander at the roots of an aspen tree. Oh! What a wonderful thing! Coyote begged Rabbit to teach him the trick. Beg beg beg, went whiny Coyote, on and on. So finally Rabbit said: "Fine, I'll teach you the trick." But he made Coyote promise not to overuse the trick, not to use it frivolously. No more than just a few times per day!

Coyote did the kind of leaping up we've all seen coyotes do, a little arched jump of joy, and he promised.

Pretty soon Coyote got the hang of things. Boy was he happy! He started to throw his eyeballs around willy-nilly, peering at whatever shiny thing caught his attention. Look over there! To the left! To the right! Up down and all around! Coyote was so proud of himself that he chucked his eyeballs high up into a tree, just to see what he might see.

Well that was that.

His eyeballs didn't come down.

He called to them and then he called again and again, but his eye sockets just ached and oozed and his world stayed black. Coyote moped around, crying and crying, asking everyone and everything to feel sorry for him. Eventually Buffalo got tired of Coyote's whinging. Buffalo, being a pretty generous fellow, said "Gawd, Coyote, if it'll make you quiet down a bit, I'll give you one of my eyeballs." Coyote was jubilant, shoving Buffalo's huge eyeball into his socket right away, the light of sky and blue of evening flooding back into his world on the left-hand side. What did it matter that the eyeball was too big for Coyote's socket, that Buffalo's eyeball protruded out a bit and sometimes popped out when Coyote sneezed? At least there was more than blackness.

Coyote was so pleased with the results of his whining and carrying on that he cried still more and harder, feeling even sorrier for himself. It was even harder having only half a world!

Lo and behold, Mouse felt sorry for him. She offered Coyote a second eye. Coyote was thrilled, snatching up the tiny little eyeball of Mouse and chucking it into his right eye socket. Suddenly Coyote's world was full and bright with light again, the horizon stretching out all around him on all sides. Coyote was so happy he ran off and didn't bother to look back. Still, he sees the world from a two-eyed perspective.

What was your oldest son's response to the story? I ask you.

Oh, you know, you say. This and that. He's worried about what to do with all the inventory in the store, all the snowboarding gear that's not selling now it's spring. The ex-girlfriend took the vacuum cleaner when she left and said "go fuck yourself" when the topic of that month's mortgage payment was broached. So now he's a month behind things, living in a dusty house where the dog hair is piling up everywhere. And boy oh boy is he pissed that I won't lend him ten grand to see him through things, you laugh.

The thing is, you say as you light another smoke, as we come closer and closer to Sunday morning, the night after I told him the story, I dreamed of Coyote again.

In the dream, you say, I am walking with my youngest son along a narrow bridge built across a desert, one of those deserts like the kind you see in *National Geographic* magazine or in advertisements for expensive Italian sports cars. Salty and cracked, white clay ground meeting white clouded sky, shimmering heat just kinda smearing everything into one shimmering glob.

I'm walking along this bridge, in a single line, with all sorts of other people, all kind of unbalanced and awkward, when suddenly there is screaming and yelling. Far off at the front of the line. People start trying to turn around, shoving and pushing. Someone falls off the bridge. I don't even see what happens to them when they fall, you say. Panic is everywhere. I catch the arm of someone trying to run backwards and I ask what's wrong. There's a rabid coyote at the end of the bridge, the person yells, wild-eyed with fright. The coyote is snapping and snarling, tearing into the flesh of especially children — we have to turn this line around!

Then, in your dream, you are suddenly at the head of the line, where the bridge slopes down from the edge of desert into a grove of trees. Your youngest son is a baby again, balanced on your hip. Sure enough, there is a huge coyote there, snarling. You see instantly that she is pregnant and when she's not snarling, she is panting. Heaving, really, her guts hanging low and her teats all swollen, leaking. So you reach out your hand. The giant she-coyote sniffs you.

Then she turns away, disappearing from view.

You can still feel the wet smear of the animal's nose on your hand. Even though it's been two days since the dream. Even though it was only a dream.

Slow as sin, you say. It's been slow as sin gettin' rid of that cool wet feeling on my hand.

Sunday morning is coming. Coming at the edge of this night.

After that you leave my house because it's dark by then and the high pitch smell of new grass that has only seen the sky for just a few days has faded as the temperature drops again into night. I hear the sound of your rental car starting up in the driveway out in front of my house. I find an old soup tin to put on the porch's railing for you to use as an ashtray the next time you come over. So you don't have to flick your still burning filters out across the lawn. I know you are driving home to an empty house, that you might call one of your sons before you go to sleep. Sunday morning will come down on you too.

I am thinking of the wet feel on your palm, a coyote's snout touching you in your dream. Staying with you into the waking hours, stretching across the membrane of night and morning, from one day until the next and then the next after that. I think about waking up tomorrow morning, Sunday morning, the way our dreams reach out wet and real into the day, the way loneliness and lessons of loss sit with us, splitting open our worlds, Coyote and his two-eyed seeing.

One Saturday night more than a decade ago now I went to sleep and world was just the way it had been for so many Saturday nights before. Then I woke up the next morning, on a Sunday, and that specific Sunday morning came down and the world was entirely new.

A world cleaved. Two-eyed seeing.

February 11th, 2001 was a Sunday. Cast your mind back.

Imagine a winter Sunday in northern British Columbia, a Sunday morning when the sky is bright bright splintered-blue cold, ready to snap. Maybe it's even below minus forty because the snow squeaks, which we know because about half an hour ago we called in our dog for his breakfast and sure enough the snow emitted sounds like an ungreased gerbil's wheel when the dog ran toward us, a great big malamute with blue eyes who seems oblivious to the freezing pain we feel upon inhaling into our own lungs the same air he's breathing, gulping as he runs toward the back door.

When we got him the woman at the animal shelter made jokes about him being some wild wolf, or maybe part coyote, and we rolled our eyes thinking that everyone up here in the north likes the idea that their dogs have some wildness part in them. We might have slept in that morning, since it was Sunday, but a siren woke up the dog just as the sun began to rise and then the dog began to howl in unison with the pitch of an emergency vehicle and soon all the dogs on our street were howling too, ramping up their calls like they were feeling empathy or something, like they were mourning, calling into the freezing not-quite-light morning air, crying for some stranger in an ambulance.

Way back then I knew nothing about Coyotes who saw the world with two different eyes.

Way back then I am living with a man who is now long gone but with whom, way back then and after we let the dog in, I made coffee and toast and then, with the dog in tow, headed back to bed with to read the weekend newspaper. We've pulled the curtains open and the sky's gotten even brighter, bluer, and colder. The dog has flopped down at the end of the bed and it is a Sunday morning so alike so many other Sunday mornings that it is all perfectly usual and there is nothing remarkable at all about it.

The phone beside the bed, which is a normal place for a phone and a place so many people have a phone, rings and the man whom I've shared a bed with for more than ten years picks it up, saying the most normal of things: Hello.

Because it's still a normal Sunday, the kind you don't remember details about. I don't remember what happened after he said 'hello' but before he passed the phone over to me. What I remember is actually *being* passed the phone, it coming toward me, me putting down the newspaper and taking care not to spill my cup of coffee as I take the receiver. It seems strange I can't remember if he had some sort of conversation on the phone, but I don't.

I just remember, "It's John: He wants to talk with you."

John is my best friend's father. A quiet man, an engineer who spent his entire career planning highways, charting load-bearing weights for bridges that still span some of the largest rivers in British Columbia. These are bridges designed specifically to outlast human life.

Once, when we were about fourteen, my best friend and I compared notes about our dads, trying to think about their most interesting characteristics. This is the kind of mindless things done by fourteen-year-old friends in small northern towns with railway tracks down the centre, towns ringed by clear-cuts and marked by avalanches and high rates of teenage pregnancy, the kind of forgettable things that go alongside learning to smoke hash, comparing notes about making out with boys, chucking stones from overpasses at logging trucks, and planning how to leave or who you're for sure going to marry. There are so many forgettable things that best friends do that most of them are forgotten exactly because they are forgettable. As long as more things happen, the fact that so much is forgotten doesn't matter. Details disappear. They die because more are born. What is worth remembering about stealing two entire bags of chocolate chips from someone's mother's kitchen and eating them all while dancing around the living room in your underwear, listening to your parents' Simon and Garfunkel records, promising each other you would never, ever, tell another soul that it was this, and not vomiting up Silent Sam vodka at a gravel pit party, that really made you happy?

I don't remember what I put forward as my dad's strong points, but she said she admired her dad for overcoming a speech impediment that resulted in a slight stutter, a stammer, every time he picked up the phone and before he could say "Hello." It was true — every time I phoned their house, if John picked up I was greeted first with silence, as if the line had gone dead, before there was an "Ahhh, yes? Hello? John here?" Always posed like a question, an inquiry as opposed to an announcement or an invitation.

Imagine being in an office all day long for work, you observed, when you answered the phone like that. You gotta admire that. From my teenage vantage point, I agreed.

So on that Sunday morning I remember saying "Hi John" and waiting through the silence, because that was normal too, although it did seem a little strange that my best friend's father was calling on a weekend morning. He said hello, and then there was a pause and so I rushed in to fill the gap and I asked him how he was doing and although I heard what he said next, there is no way to hear, to really *hear*, what I heard, so what remains in memory is something like a rush, a sucker punch to the gut, like being unexpectedly under water or having your ear pressed again the side of a metal bucket full of gravel that someone is shaking hard back and forth, a dull ache of no sound static where you hear your own breath being drawn into your own lungs and then expelled, your own heart beating.

"I'm not doing so well," says John.

"Theresa is dead."

My eyes abandon me. The world splits in two. Dogs howl. They howl for the dead, they howl for everything that was just the way it was seconds before this moment and they howl for everything that can never be the same after those three words. The brittle blue sky remains a brittle blue sky.

February 11ᵗʰ, 2001. When Sunday morning came down. *There's nothing, short of dying, that's as lonesome as the sound of Sunday morning coming down.*

Why does the earth still turn on its axis? Why is the sun rising higher in the sky? Everything should halt. Should come to a standstill. Should curl inwards onto itself, wail itself into extinction. Our dog lifts his head. The phone is back in its cradle. No. NO! Don't touch me don't touch me don't touch me, my skin a crackling salt scarred ground, snarling snapped at bitten. There is panic up ahead. Some angry terrified animal.

How can a twenty-eight-year-old woman — perfectly healthy, dark hair, crooked fingers, chipped front tooth, wandering right eye, small breasts, down-to-the-quick-bitten fingernails, bony collar bones, sensitive gums, narrow feet, piercings on one ear grown over, never could whistle very well — cease to exist. I remember us spread out on our backs under an August sky on a beach watching a meteor shower then a few weeks later the northern lights; I remember collecting stones on rivers. picking armfuls of daffodils from city parks with 'leave flowers for all to enjoy' signs, smoothing out our prom dresses, signing yearbooks, going off to college, taking the bus, holding protest signs, blockading multinational companies, marching at take-back-the-night, angst-ridden over shaving our legs, losing our grandmothers, making tea, holding each other, crying with each other, sobbing, hearts broken, breaking. Where are you when I need you right now, need you most, sobbing where does a life go, how can she be dead?

If we throw our eyes around and about without care, we will go blind. It's as if everything I have ever seen was never, really, witnessed. I am not seeing anything. My eye sockets ache. I vomit. I eat. I vomit. There is no way to see the world anew.

What had I ever seen before the moment I learned I would never see you again, alive?

There is a funeral. The worst kind of funeral imaginable: two parents are speaking about the life, and then the death, of their child. Do we remember her smile? Do we remember that she was beautiful? Do we know how much she was loved? All words are failures. Nothing correct can be voiced. Children are born to outlive their parents. By the time children are almost thirty, this seems inevitable. Parents are already sure of their own mortality, turning to their offspring to witness a separate and new independent adulthood taking hold.

Children are not meant to be buried by their parents.

It is our duty as children to do this for our parents: they bear us, we bury them. Not the other way around.

I do not dream of coyotes.

Instead, I dream of my best friend.

For years. Even today. At first I dream of her body, her always-being-autopsied-body because there is no reason found for her death, her waking-up-slightly-light-headed-and-dying-six-hours-later death. In these dreams her skin is the inside of an abalone shell, pale green shimmering with shots of blue and purple swimming underneath. She is sliced open, from top of pubis to somewhere just under the trachea, skin pulled back so fleshy flaps rest against both hip bones, against the inside curve of both breasts, a cavity of velvety red, my best friend on a steel autopsy table.

This is what fills my dreams in the nights that follow close to the day of her death.

I try calling to my eyes — come down, come back, stop looking there! Come back and be my own eyes! I will see everything carefully, I will be careful, please make her not dead, give me back my eyes. Give me back the way they saw the world before such a death.

My eyes don't listen to me. They shift into dreams where I see her. Alive. In a red jacket. I know it's her! Always far away, down a crowded city street across a public square in some foreign country riding an escalator going down when I'm going up in a mall with a blue tag sale and thousands of shoppers packed in. I spend my nights chasing her, never catching up, exhausted. Or, once, I'm a hotel in the middle of a rain forest, thick moss everywhere and a flashing neon sign incongruous when she phones: Look, she says matter-of-factly, I need you to come and get me. I'm just down the road. In the house with the tin roof and the ivy.

I'm coming I'm coming I'm running I'm calling people, her parents, I'm breathless, she's alive, it's all been a mistake, she's alive, I'll bring her home, it's all been a mistake. I get to the house, the tin-roofed house with the ivy.

She has just left says the woman who opens the door at my knock. She's just left.

When I awake I cannot shake the cool wet feeling that coats my body. I have been running all night, sweating. Even though it was just a dream, the feeling is slow to lift. An imprint of something I have touched in a dream. You in a dream touching me, *Sunday morning coming down.*

I am calling out to you. Listen! Don't leave! I want to see the world with you in it. My eyes are casting around. The sky is arching, touching down against a tree branch. There is no dream that is not a dream of you, there is nothing that I see which is not also a seeing of you.

A hawk is there, somewhere, a rabbit, a mouse. Everything impossibly small, a split second, is monumental. The ground never stops shuddering. As if herds of huge migrating animals — caribou, buffalo — were rushing across it, hooves pitting grass, dust clouds blinding.

I would tell you everything. I would give you my eyes.

The world is split.

I am sure there is a wild dog crying, a she-coyote heaving, snapping at hollow air, her belly full of pups; they will leap when they inhale the world, all of it so alive. Some prairie grass, some warm fleck of soil seen only by an insect. When I cry from missing you, thinking of you clothed in a casket of wood, the world shakes in my guts. The last thing I remember of you alive is sitting in my living room telling me about a dream, our dog resting at your feet. We are in northern British Columbia, as autumn is coming to a close. Everything is howling. I call to my eyes. Let me see you again. Let the split second that split the world be put back. Let nothing be mislaid, let nothing be gone. I want to hold on. It is impossible. I have dreamed of you on an autopsy table. No Sunday morning can ever come again without you dying, each and every morning that I awake there is a split second during which it is possible you have not died and then that second is swallowed with light and a new day begins, my eyes adjusting to the day from the night.

Sunday morning comes down.

I wish I could have told you the story I learned about Coyote.

I wish I could tell you how you are my way of seeing the world.

Everything split between when you were alive.

And now.

ACKNOWLEDGEMENTS

Essays in *Where It Hurts* have been published in a number of journals, magazines, and anthologies. I am grateful to *PRISM International* (for publishing "Soft Shoulders"), *subTerrain Magazine* (for publishing "Aesop" and "After Paul Auster Spoke About Lightning"), to *EnRoute Magazine* (for publishing both "Columbus Burning" and "Quick-Quick. Slow. Slow." as part of their ongoing commitment to the CBC Literary Awards), and to TightRope Books, who (re)published "After Paul Auster Spoke About Lightning" in *Best Canadian Essay 2014*, edited by Christopher Doda. Many thanks also to the jurors of the National Magazine Awards, the Western Magazine Awards, and the CBC Literary Prize, each of whom put my writing in some of the best writerly company this country has to offer.

I am also grateful to The Banff Centre's 2009 Wired Writing Program. This book began, in many ways, with the mentorship and unparalleled guidance of Sid Marty, an extraordinary essayist and creative non-fiction author willing to provide generous and rigorous feedback on the writing of others.

For the third time around (!), I'm thankful to the amazing team at NeWest Press, especially Anne Nothof who has a dedication to detail that I've never before had the pleasure of receiving from any editor.

Finally, I am grateful to Stephen Hume, without whom I would never have discovered creative non-fiction.

PHOTO: MARY DE LEEUW

Sarah de Leeuw holds a Ph.D. in historical-cultural geography and is currently an Associate Professor with the Northern Medical Program at UNBC, the Faculty of Medicine at the University of British Columbia, where she works in medical humanities and the determinants of marginalized peoples' health.

De Leeuw grew up on Vancouver Island and Haida Gwaii (The Queen Charlotte Islands), then lived in Terrace, BC. She earned a BFA from the University of Victoria, after which she spent time teaching English in South Korea. She also worked as a tug boat driver, women's centre coordinator, logging camp cook, and a journalist and correspondent for *Connections Magazine* and CBC Radio's *BC Almanac*. She returned to northern BC after spending four years in Ontario and another year in Arizona as a visiting Fulbright Scholar with the University of Arizona.

Her first book, *Unmarked*, was published in 2004. Her second, *Geographies of a Lover*, arrived in Spring 2012 and won the Dorothy Livesay Poetry Prize for the best book of poetry in

British Columbia that year. For two consecutive years, Sarah de Leeuw was honoured in the Creative Nonfiction category of the CBC Literary Awards, winning first place for "Columbus Burning" in 2009, and second place for "Quick-quick. Slow. Slow." in 2010. In 2013, her essay "Soft Shoulder" earned a Western Magazine Gold Award.

She currently divides her time between Prince George and Kelowna, BC.